SRPUHI DUSSAP

MAYDA

ECHOES *of* PROTEST

A Novel

TRANSLATED BY
Nareg Seferian

EDITED BY
Lisa Gulesserian

with Barbara Merguerian, Joy Renjilian-Burgy,
Judith A. Saryan, *and* Danila Jebejian Terpanjian

WITH AN INTRODUCTION BY
Valentina Calzolari

AIWA PRESS

Armenian International Women's Associa
Boston, Massachusetts

This publication was made possible by a generous grant from the Dolores Zohrab Liebmann Fund

Cover Painting: "Reading the Letter" (oil on canvas) by Thomas Benjamin Kennington (1856–1916). Private Collection. © Christopher Wood Gallery, London, UK/Bridgeman Images

Design by Taline Boghosian
© 2020 by AIWA Press
Armenian International Women's Association, Inc.
65 Main St., #3A, Watertown, Massachusetts 02472
www.aiwainternational.org

MAYDA

Contents

Srpuhi Dussap, by photographer Kevork Abdullah

Biography

Srpuhi Dussap: First Armenian Feminist

T he publication of the novel *Mayda**, by the pioneering
Armenian writer Srpuhi Dussap**, caused a sensation in
the Armenian community of Constantinople (Istanbul) in 1883.
One of the earliest books written in the Western Armenian language, based on the spoken language of the people rather than
the classical form that had been until then considered the only
acceptable written text, it offered a prose that was simple, direct,
and easily understood. Not only was it the first book to have been
written by an Armenian woman, it also was the first comprehensive Armenian text to provide a sharp critique of the unequal and
unjust position of women in contemporary society. In particular,
its declaration of the right of a woman to be well educated, to
become gainfully employed, to relate with the opposite sex on

---

* Pronounced as My-da.
** Transliterated into Eastern Armenian as Srbuhi Tiwsab, or sometimes Tyussab.

the basis of mutual respect, and to have an independent role in society was condemned by some as a threat to the fabric of traditional Armenian society. On the other hand admirers praised its ideas as a forward step in the progress and enlightenment of the Armenian nation.

The book's author, Srpuhi Vahanian Dussap, was born on February 2, 1841, in the Istanbul suburb of Ortaköy, into a wealthy and socially prominent family. Her father died when she was less than a year old, leaving her and her older brother in the care of their mother, Nazli Vahanian. Exceptionally enlightened for a woman of her time, Nazli saw to it that both of her children were well educated. She also participated fully in the rich intellectual life of the Armenian community, which was experiencing a cultural renaissance. Noted as a founder of the St Hripsimiants Girls School in 1859 and the Women's Philanthropic Association in 1864, she went on in 1879 to chair the newly established Association of Women Dedicated to Schools, whose main purpose was to educate young Armenian women to go out and teach in the Armenian villages and rural areas.

Srpuhi Dussap received her elementary education at a French private school and later was tutored by her older brother Hovhannes, a noted scientist who had been educated in Paris and became a prominent political figure in the Armenian community and, later, in the Ottoman Government, where he held key positions in the Commerce, Education, and Justice Ministries. By the age of 12, Srpuhi had read Plutarch's *Lives* and was fluent in Italian and Greek, as well as French, and it is said that as an adult she was familiar with the major classical writers, such as Plato, Aristotle, Homer, Sophocles, Euripides, and Vergil. She was well read also in the works of contemporary European authors, especially the women, such as George Sand and Katherine Adam. The United States was not outside her realm of interest; in the Preface to *Mayda* she praises America as the cradle of liberty.

It was not until she had reached her twenties, however, that Srpuhi become seriously interested in the Armenian language. This was a subject of intense controversy between the conservative elements of society, who wanted to preserve the classical language (known mainly by scholars and the clergy) as the only written form, and the progressives, who advocated development of the spoken language into a literary form readily accessible to a broader audience. Dussap's interest in the Armenian language was aroused after she met, and began to take language classes from, the well-known Armenian poet Mgrdich Beshigtashlian. With his encouragement, she began writing poetry in classical Armenian, one of her first publications being an "Ode to Spring," which appeared in the scholarly journal *Pazmaveb*, published in Venice. Her close association with Beshigtashlian—some considered it a romance—came to an end with the poet's illness and early death, in 1868, at the age of 40. Dussap was widely praised for a sentimental elegy in classical Armenian delivered at his funeral and later published as the introduction to his collected works.

In 1871 Srpuhi married her French piano teacher, Paul Dussap, who was a musician at the Turkish Sultan's court. The couple had two children, Dorine and Edgar. Paul Dussap encouraged his wife's social and literary activities, and the couple held a salon attracting local intellectuals to discuss the cultural, political, and social issues of the day. In her Preface to *Mayda*, Srpuhi Dussap expresses gratitude to her husband "for having understood and encouraged the calling of my soul," noting that his "rich mind that wanders freely in the world of harmony . . . left me free to think and to protest."

Dussap's literary career blossomed in the decade of the 1880's, when she turned from poetry to prose. A small work, *The Spoken Armenian Language*, published in 1880, supported modern Western Armenian as a literary form. Then appeared a series of articles focusing on women's issues: "Women's Education" (1880),

"The Principle of Women's Employment" (1881), and "A Few Words about Women's Inactivity" (1881–82, published in the Turkish newspaper *Tercüman-ı Efkar* as well as the Armenian *Arevelyan Mamul* of Smyrna and *Meghu Hayastani* of Tiflis).

In her first (and best-known) work, the novel *Mayda*, Dussap presented her comprehensive analysis of the inequalities suffered by women in contemporary society and challenged women to stand up for their rights. "I am the enemy of injustice and prejudice," she writes in her Preface, "consequently I see with indignation the chains by which the female sex is bound, so that neither the speech, nor the actions, nor the movements of women are natural or true." She goes on to make it clear that her motive in writing *Mayda* was not literary: "I do not have any claims to having written a great novel," she continues, but rather "to reveal the truth in a pleasant manner."

In this epistolary novel, Dussap "reveals the truth" through the story of an attractive young widow (Mayda), who has recently lost her parents and her husband and is left in straightened circumstances to raise her daughter, Houlianée. The author's ideas are expressed through correspondence, mainly between the heroine and her friend, Madam Sira, who guides Mayda from being a helpless woman feeling sorry for herself, through the vicissitudes of a complicated and eventful romance, to become a confident and self-possessed woman not only capable of taking command of her personal life but also engaged in assisting others.

Dussap's response to criticism that her feminist ideas were undermining traditional Armenian values was not to engage in polemics with her adversaries, but rather to write two additional novels in which she expanded her ideas regarding women's rights: *Siranush* (1884) and *Araksia, gam Varzhuhin* (*Araxia, or the Teacher*, 1887).

Following the publication of these three novels, Dussap encountered difficulties in her personal life. Health problems, along with concern over the position of her husband at the Ottoman court, made it impossible for her to continue writing. In 1889, accompanied by her daughter Dorine, she went on an extended visit to Paris, where the two enjoyed the rich social and cultural life of the French capital. But Dorine had contracted tuberculosis, and soon after returning to Istanbul, she died in 1891, at the age of 19. Dussap could not recover from this crushing blow and never again wrote for publication. She withdrew from society, and passed away in 1901.

By that time Dussap had become the idol of a new generation of young educated Armenian women who were inspired by her life and ideas. One day when the young Zabel Yessayan and a friend paid an unplanned visit, Dussap welcomed them warmly and conversed with them about their interests and ideas. Upon learning that they were aspiring authors, according to Yessayan's later account of the meeting, Dussap encouraged them, while at the same time warning that "for women, the world of literature was full of many more thorns than laurels" and that "a male writer was free to be mediocre; a female writer was not."

Dussap's campaign to advance the rights of women was only one aspect of her crusade for a more just and equal society. Her disapproval of the frivolity of the upper classes was clear; both in her life and in her prose she expected the privileged to do what they could to help the disadvantaged. Following her mother's example, she was known for her charitable efforts to raise funds for philanthropic activities. Proceeds from her first book (*The Spoken Armenian Language*) were donated to her mother's Women's Philanthropic Association, in which she also played an active role. Taking advantage of her social contacts, she raised money though direct solicitation as well as by fundraising activities such as theatrical performances and the first Armenian painters exhibit in Istanbul in 1882 (the famous Armenian artist Ivan Aivazovsky donated one of his works for the cause).

While advocating universal values, above all equality, justice, and humanity, Dussap was a part of the progressive movement dedicated to advance the Armenian community through education, publications, and social participation. Her efforts for the modernization of the Armenian language were designed to spread enlightenment among the Armenian people, and there is a strong strand of nationalism in her writing. In *Mayda*, for example, the heroine takes a few poor Armenian girls into her home to teach them the Armenian language and also "encouraged their love of the Armenian nation through the stories of our old fateful glorious days." Madam Sira (who speaks for the author) extolls the Armenian language and expresses regret that, living abroad, she never hears its beautiful syllables. Later in the novel, Mayda proudly acquaints her foreign friend, the Count, with the Armenian institutions of Istanbul, praising the Armenian national hospital while at the same time omitting to mention to a foreigner its faults.

Despite the conservative criticism that she was undermining traditional Armenian values, Dussap praised motherhood and supported marriage as long as it was based on love and mutual respect, and not on a commercial arrangement between families. Her fierce advocacy of women's emancipation resulted not only from her sense of social justice, but also from the conviction that it would facilitate the nation's advancement. Why should society judge women differently from men, she asks? What evidence can be cited that men are innately superior to women and therefore enabled to rule over them, as master to slave? On the contrary, history provides evidence that women can play great and important roles whenever they are given the opportunity to act. If men and women work together in harmony, on an equal basis, and if women's abilities are fully dedicated to the effort, imagine how much more can be accomplished, in an efficient and pleasant manner, to improve society, she argues.

Thus Dussap's enlightened principles went far beyond gender equality; her ideal was a society based on justice, mutual understanding, and truth. The poor and hungry were also a subject of her concern. The privileged members of society have a duty to help the less fortunate, for example by providing education and finding employment opportunities. As noted, the heroine of *Mayda* educates a group of Armenian girls in her home, and later organizes a workshop for needy women, enabling them earn much needed income.

The modern reader may find the nineteenth century romanticism of Dussap's novel dated, the plot contrived, the characters undeveloped, and the tone didactic. But however much the novel may seem dated in its literary form, its critique of contemporary society and its concern for the enlightenment and welfare of all people is as relevant today as ever before. Its call for the equality of women socially, culturally, and economically places Dussap as the first Armenian feminist, one who inspired a new generation of talented Armenian women writers. If over the years her voice has faded away, it is no less vital today. The ideas advanced by Dussap and her followers created a rich and diverse body of literature that is relevant not only to present-day Armenians, but to all those interested in multifaceted issues regarding ethnic identity, social justice, cultural values, and the evolving roles of women in society.

—Barbara Merguerian

Introduction*

Women's Emancipation and Armenian Literature in the Ottoman Empire at the Dawn of the 20th Century

By Valentina Calzolari

I n her autobiographical novel *The Gardens of Silihdar*, the writer Zabel Yessayan (1878–1943) describes a mood of sadness and despair among her young educated friends in Constantinople (Istanbul), many of whom wanted "to escape their dull lives and do something." But they did not know what they wanted to do. Yessayan recalls that "we used to read Madame Dussap's books together, and in the work of that feminist author,

---

* This Introduction has been translated and slighted revised from a paper on "Èmancipation féminine et littérature arménienne dans l'Empire ottoman à l'aube du XX siècle," presented at a workshop *Femmes et vie publique: sors de ta chamber!* at the University of Geneva, Faculté des Lettres, 11 March 2015.

we tried to find solutions to the problems we faced." One day, Yessayan and one of her friends, in search of advice, decided to visit the pioneering Armenian author and feminist, Srpuhi Dussap, who since the tragic death of her daughter a decade earlier had retired from public life. Dussap greeted her visitors warmly and asked them many questions. Yessayan recounts:

> Hearing that I hoped to become a writer, Madame Dussap tried to warn me. She said that, for women, the world of literature was full of many more thorns than laurels. She told me that in our day and age, a woman who wanted to carve out a place for herself in society was still not tolerated. To overcome all of these obstacles, I needed to exceed mediocrity. In her words, a male writer was free to be mediocre; a female writer was not.

Far from becoming discouraged by these remarks, Yessayan and her friend were inspired by the visit and vowed to go to Europe to further their education and to become writers.[1] Countless other young Armenian women were similarly inspired to follow Dussap's example and to pursue a literary career.

Regarding the difficulties facing aspiring female authors, Srpuhi Dussap knew what she was talking about. In fact, the appearance in 1883 of her first novel, *Mayda*, provoked contrasting reactions. A true literary success that sold "like hot cakes,"[2] this novel aroused at the same time the praise of progressive spirits along with the strong criticism of its detractors. The latter warned that the model of the emancipated woman offered by Dussap in this novel could have a destabilizing effect on the entire society, corrupting the Armenian people's morals and traditions. Undeterred, Dussap went on to publish in swift succession two additional novels advancing her views: *Siranush* (1885) and *Araksia, or the Teacher* (1886).[3]

Before discussing the work of this pioneering writer, who used her pen to claim the right of women's emancipation, it may be useful to describe the position of the woman in Armenian society at the time.

The Armenians of the Romantic Era: the *Zartonk* ("Awakening")

In the nineteenth century the Armenians constituted a nation scattered between East and West: more precisely, in several Western European colonies (Venice, Paris, Amsterdam) and in the East (Calcutta, Madras, Singapore). Armenia itself was split into Eastern Armenia (divided between the Russian Empire and Persia), and Western Armenia (part of the Ottoman Turkish Empire). Numerous Armenian communities were found in the large cities of the Ottoman Empire, such as Constantinople (Istanbul), Smyrna (Izmir), and Bursa, but the heart of the community lived in the interior of the country, what the Armenians call the *yergir* (homeland), otherwise known as the provinces (or vilayets) of eastern Anatolia: Van, Bitlis, Erzurum, Mamuret-ul-Aziz, Sivas, Diyarbekir—as well as the province of Adana, in Cilicia.

The condition of the Armenians in the provinces was very different from that in the capital where, beginning in the middle of the nineteenth century, significant changes had modified the economic, social, and political landscape. This period in Armenian history is called the *Zartonk*, or "Awakening."[4] A new urban, bourgeois, social class consisting of merchants, artisans, printers, lawyers, educators, journalists, doctors, and others was formed and grew in importance, to the detriment of the class of wealthy Armenian financiers, the *amiras*, who had often been the bankers of the sultans and who until then had controlled the economic, political, and cultural life within the Armenian community. As patrons, the *amiras* had encouraged cultural development, for example by financing the opening of schools or by promoting the publication of books, but their class remained nonetheless a conservative force in Armenian society.

These economic and social changes had a profound impact on Armenian cultural life. Beginning in the mid-nineteenth century, a progressive secularization of culture took place, which could be seen, inter alia, in the development of the press and the education system. The first secular schools were opened next to parochial schools. In periodicals, the issue of the cultural renewal of the Armenian nation was raised. The question of language was asked; until that time, classical Armenian—what is called *krapar*—had been the only literary language, the vernacular being confined to oral expression. It was in the press that the first debates were aired about the modernization of the language; it was also in the press that the first articles written in modern Armenian (*ashkharapar*) appeared. The first textbooks written in the modern language were also published. Numerous translations into modern Armenian appeared, and these in turn promoted the Armenian cultural renewal of the time. By reflecting on the vocabulary to be used, translators contributed to the literary development of modern Armenian. At the same time, thanks to the works of translation, European thought and literary forms were spread increasingly.[5]

This rapid overview of the main phenomena that characterized the *Zartonk* cannot be concluded without noting that public life, especially in the capital, was marked by the creation and activity of associations: if the craftsmen organized themselves in guilds (*esnafs*), then other groups, such as the promoters of education, also came together to form organizations. In this context, associations for the encouragement of the education of young girls were created. In general, the "woman's question" began to be recognized and discussed.

In the Countryside

If, in the last decades of the nineteenth century, the question of the emancipation of women began to animate debates in the capital, the situation was very different in the countryside, where the patriarchal society evolved less rapidly and remained strongly attached to the principle of the perpetuation of the clan through the institution of marriage. Considered a contract, marriage was preceded by arrangements between families. For the woman, marriage implied a break with her family of origin. Deprived of all individuality, the bride was at the service of the continuity of the lineage of her husband. Although the exact situation varied, a wife, once entered into her husband's family, had the right to speak only after having given birth to at least one male child. This imposed regime of silence followed a very rigid code that ethnographers have termed "codified silence." One scholar has described the situation of a married Armenian woman in the Caucasus in the late nineteenth century as follows (this reflects a situation widespread not only in the Caucasus but in Anatolia too):

> The bride (*hars*) is condemned to silence. She must do the duty of the bride, that is not to say a word (and not even answer except by signs) to the mother of her husband for three years, to the father of her husband for ten to twelve years, to the wives of the brothers of her husband up to one year, to the brothers of her husband for fifteen years, to the "godfather" for twenty-five to thirty years, sometimes even until death.[6]

Nineteenth-century photographs of Armenian villagers in Anatolia frequently depict the women with a scarf over their mouths, as a sign of their silence. And in some areas, this enforced silence led the brides to develop their own sign language, known as *harsneren*, in order to communicate with each other.[7]

According to this system of values, the virginity of the fiancée and the irreproachable conduct of the bride were the necessary conditions for a woman to be accepted as the guarantor of the purity of the husband's family, as one can read in the study by Avetis Aharonian, presented in 1913 at the University of Lausanne as a thesis in the history of religions.

It is therefore not surprising that in all classes of the Armenian people a great importance is attached to the sign of virginity. Its absence can lead to a breach of contract. The proof of virginity, after the nuptial night, is shown to all female members of the family, as well as to close relatives, as an inescapable testimony to the purity of the bride.

It was up to the mother-in-law to investigate the mores and the origin of the fiancée. She was the one who welcomed the young wife into her new home; it was also she who, after marriage, watched over the conduct of her daughter-in-law and passed on the necessary knowledge to guide the domestic hearth.[8] The bride was completely subject to her absolute authority, as well as to that of the other family members:

> The woman, in the large family, enjoys no particular regard. She is even obliged to perform the bride's duty towards her husband's brother as soon as he is ten years old: not to speak to him, to take off his shoes, to satisfy all his caprices. She receives orders not only from the father of her husband, the mother of her husband, and her husband himself, but even from the older wives of her husband's brothers and her husband's brothers themselves. Without her mother-in-law's permission, she is not allowed to step outside the house.[9]

And even:

> The inner government of the large family is entirely un-
> der the authority of the mother. She governs the affairs of
> the house with unlimited power, and she is the one who
> gives orders to the daughters for the division of the work.
> Without her permission, no daughter-in-law can hold a
> key, or take the smallest piece of bread. Without her per-
> mission, the daughter-in-law has no right to go to any
> other house.

The good organization of the home depends on the distribution
of work within the household. It is considered that the smooth
running of the home is the necessary basis at higher level for the
smooth running of the entire society. The woman should stay at
home and perform the domestic duties and tasks incumbent on
her. Among these tasks, she must light and keep the fire of the
tonir (the buried oven that was at the heart of each house): "The
woman has her particular place next to the fire, where as mother
and mistress of the house she is its vigilant guardian. She has the
daily obligation to maintain it." The smoke coming out of the
fireplace is considered the visible sign of a home that is well run,
as depicted in one of Aharonian's stories.[10]

In his dissertation, devoted mainly to ancient beliefs in
Armenia and their survival in the Armenians' contemporary
morals and customs (between the nineteenth and twentieth centuries), Aharonian compared the Armenian woman to the "vestal
virgin of the home." Inspired by *The Ancient City* by Fustel de
Coulanges (published in Strasbourg in 1864), he attributed a
sacred value to the hearth based on an analogy with the ancient
cult of the hearth of people of Indo-European origin, in particular
the Romans and Greeks, to whom he compared the Armenians.
As keeper of the fire of the *tonir*, the Armenian woman was, for

Aharonian, the priestess of the hearth itself. In the purity of the hearth, preserved uncontaminated, could be found the continuity of what this author called the "Armenian pagan soul" and "the heart of the nation."[11]

The principle of preserving the family against any danger of contamination is upheld under different forms of prohibition. For example, marriage with a foreign woman is forbidden. In this respect, the situation of the countryside does not differ from that of the cities, as can be seen, for example, in *The Gardens of Silihdar*, in which Zabel Yessayan recalls the exclusion to which her uncle had been condemned after his marriage to a Greek woman, a marriage that her grandmother pardoned only much later, in her old age. Yessayan also recalls that her paternal aunt Annig did not allow any of her children to marry, for fear of seeing a stranger enter the family:

> Of my four aunts, I only knew Annig—a tyrannical woman who kept all her adult children under strict orders not to marry. She did not want a new person entering the family and disturbing the perfect control she had established over the household.

Recalling the different attitude of her father, who married the woman he loved despite the resistance of his sisters, Yessayan noted that he had even quarreled with Annig because of his more enlightened attitude. Her father

> tried to convince her to let her daughter marry the boy she loved, which Aunt Annig thought would bring dishonor on the family. These were the customs in the capital. Simply exchanging glances or smiles was enough to ruin the reputations of young men and women, who had perhaps never even had the opportunity to speak to one

another. Until my adolescence, I remember hearing un-
mistakably denigrating remarks about young people who
had fallen in love before getting married.[12]

In the countryside as in the city, marriage for love was dis-
approved, an attitude Dussap challenged, above all in her
novel *Siranush*.

The Situation of Women in the Large Cities, Notably Constantinople

The capital however offered emancipation opportunities that
were not available to Armenian women in the countryside. The
city offered public places and opportunities, beginning with
the associations, within which women found opportunities to
express themselves and to be active in the public arena. In this
context can be seen the charitable educational associations that
worked to develop a school network and advocated the exten-
sion of education to girls. Among these associations, at least two
should be mentioned: the Women's Philanthropic Association,
founded in 1859, and the Armenian Women's Association for the
Good of the Nation, founded in 1879 in the Armenian quarter
of Scutari (today Üsküdar) in the Asian side of the city.

In addition to associations, new cultural and social salons
that some Armenian women had the opportunity to attend
played a role; these were true centers for discussion, the exchange
of ideas, and meeting, following the model of European salons.
Among others, one can recall in this connection the salons of
George Sand (1804–1876) or of Juliette Adam (1836–1936),
which Dussap frequented during a stay in Paris.

Other possibilities for expression were offered to women by
the press, which became a major arena for the dissemination of
the new trends represented by the *Zartonk*. As early as 1862,

Elbis Gesaratsian became the first female editor of the Western Armenian media when, on August 1 of that year, she began publication in Constantinople of an eight-page monthly women's newspaper called *Guitar*. In it Gesaratsian encouraged women to meet the challenges of changing conditions through education and community service, and she argued that women's rights are basic to social justice. Harshly criticized as a radical by the male-dominated press, Gesaratsian was able to publish only ten issues of *Guitar*.[13] In later decades, women's columns were created in some periodicals, and these helped to raise the consciousness of enlightened women.[14]

In this context a change began, as Yessayan and her friends, too cramped in traditional society, aspired "to escape their dull existence and do something." Yessayan writes, "They wanted to receive an education, participate in public life, go on walks with their male friends, meet in public, travel, and everything else." This spirit of "revolt" found different forms of expression. Some of them were in constant conflict with their families. Verkinee, for one, had refused to wear clothing traditionally considered appropriate for women: "She cut her hair—which was very uncommon at the time, dressed simply, and wore a man's tie." For Verkinee, these external forms were "critical to overcoming the restrictions placed on her." All of these young women "were troubled by periods of sadness and despair." The answer to this despair and to this "dull existence" was sought in literature: "We used to read Madame Dussap's books together, and in the work of that feminist author, we tried to find solutions to the problems we faced." Despite a liberal and progressive father, Yessayan herself felt the weight of the "obstacles that the backward bourgeoisie so oppressively imposed on all of us." Hence the decision by Yessayan and her friends to visit Dussap, the dean, who, despite the fact that she had retired from public life, continued to represent a figure of first rank for the young women.

Leaving Dussap's house, much impressed by this visit, Yessayan and her friends, full of enthusiasm, confided to each other their aspirations to become writers and their imperative need for higher education in Europe, in order "to exceed mediocrity." Literature was considered a form of resistance and an instrument of emancipation. For Yessayan and her friends, Dussap, though a member of the previous generation, continued to be a fundamental model from which they could draw inspiration and advice.[15]

Srpuhi Vahanian Dussap

In the space of only a few years (between 1883 and 1886), Srpuhi Dussap (born Vahanian) published the three novels that made her popular: *Mayda* (1883), *Siranush* (1885), and *Araksia* (1886). Born into a wealthy family, she was the daughter of Nazli Vahanian (1813/4–1884), founder of the Saint Hripsimé School for young girls in 1859, and the Women's Philanthropic Association in 1864. Madame Nazli was a patron of several orphanages and schools in the capital (for example the Kalfayan Orphanage and the Naregian and Hamazgiats schools). On the model of the Europeans, she held a private salon that was animated by the participation of several contemporary intellectuals and became a center for the discussion of social issues. Although widowed, she was able to provide an education to her children, thanks to her family's comfortable financial situation. Dussap received an excellent education, at first in the French school in the district of Ortaköy, where she was born—French, it should be noted, was considered as the language of elites within Ottoman society—and then with private tutoring. Her relation with her Armenian-language tutor, the poet Mgrdich Beshigtashlian (1828–1868), was the origin of her awareness of the importance of the Armenian language (ancient and modern) that she had previously scorned. One of her earliest publications was a work on "The Modern Armenian Language," and she became a champion of the movement to foster the literary use of the vernacular language against the conservatives who insisted on classical form as the only proper written version of the Armenian language. Around 1871 she married the French musician, Paul Dussap, with whom she had two children: Edgar and Dorine. She supervised their education, as her mother had hers.

Dussap began to devote herself very early to public life. With her husband, she organized musical evenings, theatrical performances, and other initiatives designed to finance, among other things, associations and schools. Among the events she promoted was the first exhibition by Armenian painters, held in Constantinople in 1882. In 1879 she became active in the Association of Women Dedicated to Schools (*Throtsaser Dignats Engerutiun*). The goal of this Association was to prepare Armenian girls for a teaching career. It cultivated particularly the plan to train future teachers who could go to the provinces remote from the capital, to promote, there too, education, especially female.

In 1880–1882, Dussap published her first articles on the situation of women: "Women's Education," "Principles of Women's Work," and "A Few Words on Women's Inactivity." [16] These are themes she would return to in her novels published a few years later: the equality of men and women; the need of meaningful work for women as well as men; the right to education; the emancipation of women to escape submission to her family and to her husband. Dussap stressed the importance of women's education; she advocated work not only as a form of women's emancipation, but also as a means of bringing about important social changes and playing a role in the progress and modernization of the nation.

It should be remembered that during the *Zartonk* era, women's emancipation already had a history in the West (France,

England, and the United States). Among the founding texts can be mentioned *A Vindication of the Rights of Women* by Mary Wollstonecraft (London, 1792) and *Declaration of the Rights of Woman and the Female Citizen* by Olympe de Gouges (Paris, 1791). The American movements of the nineteenth century must have been known to the Armenians. Beginning in Dussap's time, important works had already been published in the United States, for example the book *Woman in the Nineteenth Century* (1845) by Margaret Fuller, who called for women's independence. Feminist claims and the fight against slavery went hand in hand. It has been emphasized that a work such as *Uncle Tom's Cabin* by Harriet Beecher Stowe, published in 1852 (and issued in a translation into modern Western Armenian by the Venice Mkhitarian Press as early as 1854), helped to demonstrate the importance of women in the fight against social injustices and to pave the way for the women's rights movements that emerged in the following decades. It is interesting to note that in the Preface to her novel *Mayda*, Dussap specifically mentions America as the "cradle of liberty." A study of the foreign sources she might have read, or at least known about indirectly, would be interesting in this regard.

The First Novel: *Mayda* (1883)

The question of the development of vernacular Armenian as a literary language, which was mentioned above as among the factors in the modernization of the Armenians, is particularly relevant in assessing the publication of Dussap's first novel, *Mayda*. At the time of its publication, indeed, Western Armenian literature did not yet have a tradition. In the field of prose, in particular, there are only a few examples:[17] the first novel, *Khosrov and Makruhi* by Y. Hisarian, was published in 1851; the writer Dzerents (1822–1888) published three historical novels (in 1877–1881) set in medieval times. Matteos Mamourian (1830–1901), translator, educator, and journalist of Smyrna, had left unfinished his historical novel *The Man of the Black Mountain* (1871), set in the era of the Russo-Persian wars (1877–1878); he was the author of *Armenian Letters* (1872), inspired by Montesquieu's *Persian Letters*, and an epistolary novel *English Letters* (1881).

The innovation introduced by the publication of *Mayda* is thus significant in modern Armenian literary history. Dussap was a pioneering writer in many ways, not only because of her bold themes, but also for choosing modern Western Armenian for her literary work, a decision that was not obvious and that was taken after some hesitation.[18]

With *Mayda*, Dussap tackles the tradition of the epistolary novel, which had just been inaugurated in Armenian by Mamourian, although with different characteristics, and which had been tested especially in European literature. Written in the form of correspondence, *Mayda* gives voice to women; several female characters, through their letters, express their personal ideas and exchange their points of view. The main voice is that of Mayda, a young widow who has lost her parents and also her husband, and finds her only consolation in her daughter Houlianée. Mayda confides in an older friend, Sira, who writes to her from Corfu. It is through the voice of Sira that Dussap speaks. In this novel, the author demonstrates the condition of dependence in which the woman is found. Sira helps Mayda to understand that she had always been subject to her husband's wishes, and that she had depended on his decisions as well as her mother's advice. Now that she is alone, she finds herself unable to carry on. Her older friend advises her to stand up on her own feet, find a job, and participate in social life. Mayda meets and falls in love with a handsome bachelor, Dikran, and the remainder of the novel deals with the vicissitudes of their relationship.

A new model of woman enters the scene in this first novel, one who attracted strong criticism, even among the intellectuals considered the most enlightened. Krikor Zohrab (1861–1915), an Armenian lawyer who became a member of the Ottoman Parliament and one of the best known Armenian writers in the mainstream, condemned *Mayda* immediately upon its publication. In 1883, in the periodical *Yergrakunt* [Globe], he expressed concern that the desired freedom for women could corrupt the customs and traditions of the family, opening the door to social tragedies. Refusing to recognize women's equal rights, he insisted that the woman should remain home, attached to the family, and preserve her grace and beauty. On the contrary, Reteos Berberian, who was a preceptor of the celebrated Constantinople Central College, where some of the most important writers of the following generation studied, was among the Dussap's defenders. The quarrel between Berberian and Zohrab continued for several years.[19]

The strong criticism did not discourage Dussap. Her following two novels condemn with the same firmness the submission of women within the family and society, and emphasize women's right to work both as a means of personal emancipation and as a factor in the modernization of the Armenian nation. And at the same time other voices on the Armenian intellectual scene became heard on this issue. Under the influence of the sociological works of Herbert Spencer, Krikor Chilingirian (1839–1923), translator and educator from Smyrna, published in 1888 an essay entitled "Woman in the Nineteenth Century," in which he relayed women's demands and aspirations "to think, to have feelings, to act in a free way," and to be considered as social individuals. Chilingirian emphasized the importance of the role of women in public life, especially in the field of education.[20] He was one of the friends mentioned in the Preface to this novel who encouraged Dussap to write *Mayda*.

Siranush (1885)

Enclosed in her room, and in a suffocating society, the protagonist of Dussap's second novel, *Siranush*, is the victim of a marriage to an oppressive husband arranged by her family.

Not intimidated by the voices of disapproval or outrage aroused by her first novel, Dussap continued to confront, in her romantic way, several aspects of social criticism. Across the condemnation of the deplorable condition of women, it is the entire Armenian society that she denounces in *Siranush*, a society that holds the woman in submission by denying her any possibility of individual expression and that humiliates or—worse still—bruises it. In this novel, Dussap's critique goes beyond the scope of women's demands, and widens to include class. Here Dussap basically attacks Armenian conservative forces, and especially the class of *amiras* (magnates), by lending her voice to the less favored strata.

Siranush belongs to one of the wealthy Armenian *amira* families, who mutually transmitted wealth and political power, particularly through marriage. The idea of preservation, mentioned above, implied not only the prohibition of marriage with foreigners or strangers, but also a barrier between people from different social classes. Because of this, Siranush cannot marry the man she loves, Yervant, but has to bow to the choice of the family, who intends her for another *amira*, Darehian. The man she loves does not belong to this social class. He is poor, an artist besides; in order to improve his skills, he would like to go to Europe to complete his training, an ambition that, in the eyes of Siranush's family, is not considered an asset.

To express her criticism of the inaction of the *amira* class, Dussap presents Darehian as the antithesis of Yervant. Darehian has neither principles nor talent nor aspirations of elevated morality. On the contrary, he leads a dissolute life. While he himself visibly deceives and cheats on his wife, he places spies at Siranush's side to watch her constantly. The life she leads is presented as infernal. Locked up and enslaved in a closed circle, Siranush dies of consumption.

Different is the situation of another woman in the novel, Zaruhi, who belongs to a lower social class than Siranush. Paradoxically, this gives her more freedom. She can study, become a teacher, and marry the man she loves. Through analyzing parallel between the lives of Siranush and Zaruhi, Dussap criticizes the corrupt society of the *amiras*, while highlighting the merits and social importance of the less advantaged classes as forces to bring about renewal of the nation, forces whose power is based not on the possession and transmission of material goods, but on talent, study, and work. In *Siranush*, Dussap attaches particular importance to art as an element of enlightenment: Yervant is a painter, and he could be compared to the musician husband of Dussap herself, who had praised these moral qualities in Mayda.

Araksia (1886)

The importance of education and work is the core of Dussap's third novel too, *Araksia, or the Teacher* (*Araksia, gam Varjuhin*), that the writer dedicated to her daughter Dorine. In this novel, two women belonging to different generations represent two antithetical visions of the world. To provide for the material necessities of the family, Araksia wants to work. Her mother, on the contrary, considers that it would stain the honor of the family if her daughter went to work, because it would reveal their indigent situation. She puts her trust rather in the charity of a rich relative. For Araksia, work is not a mark of dishonor, but on the contrary it represents a means for the woman to assert her personality and autonomy, contribute to the needs of the home, and become a full member of society. In the article "A Few Words on Women's Unemployment," Dussap had already argued for the nobility of work, addressing women who, imbued with conventional ideas and prejudices, regarded employment as degrading. It particularly addressed widows, such as Araksia's mother, by exhorting them to secure the future of their children through their own means.

Education and occupation go hand in hand in Dussap's discourse. In this regard, it is important to distinguish two ideas about education. The traditional education of women in bourgeois social classes was designed for prestige and appearance, for no purpose other than to prove membership in an elite; it consisted of learning French, playing the piano, etc. But Dussap argues for a different kind of education, one providing women with useful skills to be able to engage in a profession. In *Araksia*, for example, the disciplines less frequently found in the traditional formation of girls, such as mathematics, are highlighted. Long passages in *Araksia* emphasize the fact that a woman is endowed not only with a heart, but also with rational faculties. It is thanks to her reading that Araksia is equipped to argue and to reply to her mother. The study of philosophy (ancient and modern), in particular, is somehow a determining element of Araksia's awareness, teaching her to "compare, examine, think." These philosophical readings "were more useful to her" than "all established habits, opinions, and prejudices." Following this realization, Araksia feels the need to be free: free to think, free to love, free to work. Also free to be able to exist as a "useful individual" to society and to loved ones. Thanks to elevated and suitable instruction, the woman represented by Dussap wants, and can legitimately aspire to, an active role in the struggle for freedom, hence its importance at the national level too.[21] To reprise the theme of this study, she wants to "get out of her room."

The Preface to *Mayda*

The role of art and artistic experience has been emphasized in the Preface to *Mayda*. Here Dussap's ringing summary of her opinions regarding women's issues is interesting on several levels. The tradition of epistolary novels often includes the presence of an introductory text, which can be written by an external narrator, often the novel's author. In *Mayda*, the first words are those of the author, who, in the Preface, explains the meaning of her approach and the motivation for her work.

This Preface is first of all a testimony of the "engaged" character of Dussap's pen. Among other aspects, the text also shows that Dussap is well aware of the pioneering nature of her literary work. When she emphasizes the imperfections of her art and the weaknesses of her story, her words should not be interpreted only as understatements, but rather as the expression of a writer conscious of entering an arena new to the Armenian literary world. The panorama of Western Armenian literature did not yet include a tradition to which Dussap could have referred.

The topics discussed were not new *outside* of the Armenian environment: Dussap mentions reading books, probably foreign, that supported her principles, while explicitly evoking the American model of freedom as well as European movements. The parallel with Western feminist movements will be explicit in women's writings of the next generation. Zabel Yessayan and Sibil (Zabel Khanjian Asadur), for example, mention "European sisters" and place them next to "Armenian sisters," that is to say women of ancient Armenian history, considered paradigms to imitate.[22]

Amidst the progressive circles that supplied the readings accessible to her and (as with *Araksia*) contributed to her awareness, Dussap opposes the conservative environment that obliged her to silence. The Preface insistently contrasts the theme of the voice and the silence. In light of Dussap's criticism of the negation of woman's individuality and the codified silence imposed upon her, this emphasis acquires a particular significance. It is within the family—with her mother at first and her husband later—that Dussap claims to have found decisive encouragement to continue her thoughts and plans, emphasizing the role of mother-to-daughter transmission, on the one hand, and praising the spirit of her artist husband, on the other.

According to Dussap, the role of the family in the development of her work and her approach is indisputable. Her position in a family that could be described as not only progressive, but also of a high social class, provided her with a kind of rampart. Writing many years later, in 1952, in her autobiography *On the Road of My Life*, the writer Zaruhi Kalemkerian (1874–1971) observed that Dussap was able to put forth proposals considered so radical by contemporary society only because of her wealth and high social status; a women of middle-class background writing in the same vein would have been severely condemned for expressing such ideas.

On the other hand, considering the urban environment in which the plot and the characters of the three novels are placed, Arpiar Arpiarian (1851–1908), a writer of the "realism" school, objected that the woman represented by Dussap could not be a model of an Armenian woman, but, at most, a prototype based on the urban woman of Constantinople. For him, the real woman would be found in the countryside: "The Armenian woman is found in the Armenian soil, and whoever wants to defend her cause must first study her life by living with her." With good reason, Victoria Rowe points to the irony of a man telling a woman that he is better qualified than she to define the essence of a true Armenian woman. The objection of not having written plausible stories was also addressed to her later by the writer and literary critic Hagop Oshagan (1883–1947). In any event, Dussap did not aim to write a novel of realistic inspiration, but rather to suggest that the examples offered by the European romantic tradition were relevant to the progress of the Armenian people.[23] It could be interesting to study Dussap's literary clichés and the way in which she put them to the service of her audacious writing.

Without dwelling on the discussion and criticism surrounding Dussap's novels by writers of her generation and later, it is important to note that underlying these debates is the question, among other things, of research (or the illusion of being able to conduct research) about what is "really" Armenian, let alone what could be considered a "real" Armenian woman. One wonders, in particular, whether it is only in the countryside of Anatolia, the *yergir*, that can be found those who can be considered authentically Armenian.

As a conclusion

It cannot be overemphasized that a correct appreciation of Srpuhi Dussap's work cannot exclude the dimension that could be called national. Several formulas could be used to characterize the novelistic work of Dussap: expression of social demands; literary experimentation in a vernacular language that tries to be free from the tyranny and forms of the classic Armenian language; original "translation" of Western literary forms and thought into the Armenian literary landscape in its infancy; means of propelling the (voice of) the woman on the public scene; instrument to denounce the injustices suffered by women and by the less well-off in society; etc. All of the aspects that characterize the totality of Dussap's novels should be considered as part of the nineteenth century "awakening" of the Armenians. Although the national theme is not explicit—there is no mention, for example of national liberation—Dussap's work encompasses many aspects of the more general quest of the Armenian community in the Ottoman Empire as it attempted to emancipate itself and to construct itself, or at least to think of itself, as a nation.

Endnotes for Introduction

1. Zabel Yessayan, *The Gardens of Silihdar*, translated by Jennifer Manoukian (Boston: AIWA Press, 2014), 134–36.

2. Shuraryan, Albert S., *Srpuhi Dussap: Her Life and Work* (Yerevan State University, 1963, 128 [in Armenian]; cited in Eddie Arnavoudian, "Why we should read . . . *Srpuhi Dussap*" (http://www.groong.org/tcc/tcc-20030519.html).

3. On Srpuhi Dussap, see Victoria Rowe, *A History of Armenian Women's Writing, 1880–1922* (London: Gomidas Institute, 2009), especially pages 47–89. Also, Azadouhi Simonian Kalaidjian, "Serpuhi Vahanian Dussap: Defining a New Role for Women," in *Voices of Armenian Women*, edited by Barbara Merguerian and Joy Renjilian-Burgy (Boston: AIWA Press, 2000), 162–78.

4. On the *Zartonk*, see the brief and useful synthesis by Boghos L. Zekiyan, *The Armenian Way to Modernity: Eurasiatica* 49 (Venice: Supernova, 1997).

5. Marc Nichanian, *Âges et usages de la langue arménienne* (Paris: Entente Press, 1989), 266–304.

6. Ethnographer Yervant Lalayan published his observations made among the Armenians of Javakh (present-day Georgia) in 1896 and 1897; they are reprinted in Lalayan's *Works*, Vol. 1 (Yerevan: Armenian Academy of Sciences, 1983) [in Armenian]. Observations here are quoted from Jean-Pierre Mahe, "Structure sociale et vocabulaire de la parenté et de la collectivité en arménien contemporain" in *Revue des Études Arméniennes*, 18 (1984), 327–45.

7. See the interesting work by Carla Kekejian, who conducted fieldwork in 2016 in the Tavush Province of present-day northeast Armenia, where she interviewed elderly villagers who remembered this sign language. The first and only previous study of *harsneren* was conducted in the early 1930s by the Georgian scholar D. P. Karbelashvili (https://csw.ucla.edu/2017/03/14/harsneren-language-armenian-bride/).

8. Avétis Aharonian, *Les anciennes croyances arméniennes* (Marseille: Éditions Parenthèsis, 1980), 14–15 (originally published in Geneva in 1913).

9. Lalayan, *Works*, 344–45.

10. Aharonian, *Anciennes croyances*, 17. See also Aharonian's *Sur le chemin de la liberté* (Marseille: Éditions Parenthèsis, 2006), 47–54 (originally published in 1926).

11. Aharonian, *Anciennes croyances*, 10–11. For an analysis of this aspect of Aharonian's work and its relation to Fustel de Coulanges, see Valentina Calzolari, "À la recherche de 'l'âme païenne' des Arméniens: Avétis Aharonian, *Les anciennes croyances arméniennes* (1913) et *La Cité antique* de Fustel de Coulanges (1864)" in Aram Mardirossian, Agnès Ouzounian, Constantin Zuckerman (dir.), *Mélanges Jean-Pierre Mahé* (*Travaux et mémoires* 18), Paris: Association des Amis du Centre d'Histoire et Civilisation de Byzance, 127–44.

12. Yessayan, *Gardens*, 13–15.

13. Sona Zeitlian, "Pioneers of Women's Journalism in the Western Armenian Media, 1868–1962" in *Voices of Armenian Women*, 120.

14. See Rowe, *Armenian Women's Writing*, 149–87.

15. Yessayan, *Gardens*, 134–35.

16. An English Translation by Jennifer Manoukian as "Women's Inactivity" was printed in *The Armenian Weekly*, Dec. 28, 2013.

17. Very different was the situation of Eastern-Armenian literature (in the Caucasus and Persian Armenia), where the novel asserted itself as the literary genre in prose par excellence, thanks to authors such as Khachadur Abovian, the very prolific Raffi, and others.

18. The first version of the book was probably written in French. Krikor Chilingirian, who encouraged Dussap to write in Armenian, supervised the Armenian edition. See Sharuryan, *Dussap*, 97–99.

19. For Zohrab's criticism, as well as Berberian's defense, see Rita Vorperian, "A Feminist Reading of Krikor Zohrab," A dissertation submitted in partial satisfaction of the requirements for the degree Doctor of Philosophy in Near Eastern Languages and Cultures, University of California, Los Angeles, 1999, especially 103–9.

20. Krikor Chilingirian, "Woman in the Nineteenth Century" (1888), translated into English in Agop J. Hacikyan, ed., et al., *The Heritage of Armenian Literature*, vol. III (Detroit: Wayne State University Press, 2005), 367–71.

21. Rowe, *Armenian Women's Writing*, 71–77.

22. Ibid., 47–50.

23. Ibid., 53–54.

Mayda

Author's Preface

I was still quite young when I began to read authors who protest strongly against social and religious abuse. Those protests were echoed in my heart, they were ever on my mind, and I was particularly encouraged by my mother's progressive and serious ideas through which she had long been shining over the conservative world of the Armenian nation. Nothing is as powerful as a mother's inspiration. And so, an enmity toward abuse and a love for justice would grow in me—but a powerless and speechless love, for the circles in which I lived would condemn me to silence.

Finally the day came when my companion in fortune turned out to be a son of the arts—that is, a son of infinity, for the arts are boundless. The rich mind that wanders freely in the world of harmony, being the natural enemy of limited circles and prejudices, left me free to think and to protest. Today, I publicly declare my gratitude to my husband for having understood and encouraged the calling of my soul and for having continued in a manner my mother's role.

And so for some time now my soul has been consumed by the sight of several kinds of pitiable social prejudices. I would see things that would pain me, I would protest in speech, and today I protest in writing. What does my lack of power matter to me? What do trials matter? I am obedient to the voice of my conscience, I fulfill a need. That is enough for me.

I repeat—I am the enemy of injustice and prejudice. Consequently, I see with indignation the chains by which the female sex is bound, such that neither the speech, nor the actions, nor the movements of women are natural or true. And could truth ever live under a yoke? The painful condition of women has always been the subject of my reflections, for the woman is the pitiful victim of society. She is ashamed of loving—that is, of confessing that she has a heart. She is ashamed of uttering the word "justice"—that is, of manifesting that she has a right. She is ashamed of revealing the abuses of religion and the laws—that is, of demonstrating that she has a conscience and reason. Finally, she is ashamed to fully display her moral state, to say, "It is I, I too can be reckoned with." And so, she lives head lowered, her palm covering her mouth, she passes from this world voiceless and noiseless, and the more imperceptible her conduct, the more praiseworthy it will be.

Behold our current painful state of affairs, against which great America—the cradle of liberty—protests, and whose protests are beginning to find their echoes in Europe, strengthening day by day.

I wished to mark the main social abuses by way of a romantic story. Consequently, I do not claim to having written a great novel or even one of moderate perfection. I wanted to reveal the truth in a pleasant manner, and this became my main stimulus for writing a novel—although I confess that I was encouraged to create this work by wise and indulgent friends whose voices have always influenced me.

I request the forgiveness of my readers regarding my work. If it is deprived of perfection, it has at least this one advantage, that the truth is expressed in it with conscientious bravery. I know that some will be hurt, others will become indignant, and many will consider me daring. The pen should be the instrument of truth. What does it matter if it is persecuted and condemned? After all, is not truth a sublime martyrdom?

—Srpuhi Dussap

Mme Sira to Mayda

So you say that death treated you with pitiless cruelty, viciously snatching your father, your mother, and your husband.

We humans are born into the cornucopia of mankind, and we die to enrich the vast fields of death with our ashes. Birth and death are the two poles of life—one begins what the other ends. Unwittingly, we serve their purposes—whether alive or dead, we are each part of an organic whole. Death strikes by chance, choosing its victims randomly. It cares not at all for those caught in its crosshairs! We are born, we flourish, and we die only to create room for those to come. If we see a few more suns, that's all fine and good. But does death give a damn when all it cares about is adding to its pile of booty? Yes, you fell into death's hands and it pummeled you with its blows. And yet death didn't strike you because of who you are, but because you just happened to be there at the wrong time.

So you say that fortune, which has favored you since the cradle, ended up as your enemy in the end. But what is fortune if not the way things turn out? The glorious bouquet of life is made up of both flowers and thorns, and this bouquet is constantly shedding and regenerating itself. You received the flowers first, but then you were pricked by its thorns. That's the whole story in a nutshell.

Your loved ones lived and died, while you remained—is that so surprising? Someday, your turn will come, and perhaps you will abandon others as you were abandoned. You were left without the comfort of your mother's unlimited, tireless devotion, without her watchful gaze to shelter you and your maidenly charms. You were left without the protection of your father to watch you bloom, like a delicate plant. You were left without the support of your husband's love. You were left with nothing, nothing except ruins. But instead of focusing on the rubble, construct a new edifice with the remnants! Gather the feelings once lavished on you and shower your daughter with them! Love her as your mother loved you, and be the protector of your daughter as her father would have been! Double your love, and your place and worth will double equally. Children grow in accordance with our care, and if all goes well, they will reward our sacrifices in kind. If we lose a vulnerable child to motherly negligence, that child will go on to abandon you and others in the future. Wrongdoing bears fruit—its poison saps the root.

You say that the only thing you see on the horizon is a black mark of death. Stop focusing on it! Turn instead toward another, brighter spot—the arc of the future was never meant to remain shrouded in darkness. Myriad stars of hope shimmer there with their sweet and consoling brightness. With diligence, we reveal life's brilliance. With despair, its dimness. You are free to choose between the light or the night.

———◇———

Mayda to Mme Sira

Suffering, despair, and darkness—these are my lot in life. Tears and sighs—these are my pleasures. A rigid society—these are my parents. Already society watches and waits for me to take one wrong step so that it can condemn me and tear me to pieces. Society is a relentless judge that improves nothing. Already its whip is prepared for me. A widow is a victim deprived of an avenging voice. How should she act? What steps should she take? I am anxious and depressed. I am the verdant leaf torn from the tree by a cruel snowstorm. I'll be dragged through the dirt until I'm torn apart and my parts are scattered here and there. O my second mother, help me in my bitterest moment, lead me with your experienced counsel!

———◇———

Mme Sira to Mayda

What are you complaining about? You created this condition yourself. You backed yourself into a corner that stifled you until you screamed. You wished to overcome evil only after it had already reached its apex. You could have stifled it at the beginning, but now you are its prisoner. You embraced the world and its vices, falsehoods, and insincerities. You took pleasure there, not knowing to what you were abandoning yourself. You're terrified now that you see your monstrous condition. You complain without investigating the reason—which is you, really.

When you were a child, you lived under the protection of your parents; when you were in the full blossom of youth, that of your husband. You owed everything to your husband. You fervently protected your honor for him and through him. You owed him your life and even the name you bore, which you kept spotless in his honor. And did you have anything to show for yourself? Didn't the name of your family, your very being, your love of honor mean anything to you? You lived virtuously so as not to debase your husband's honor. You lived that way not because you are a woman or an angel, not because you wanted to keep your greatness born of virtue, not because you are a mother—that clarifying heavenly mirror in which the innocent child sees its innocent reflection.

So are you nothing on your own? Do you count for nothing, acquiring worth only when following that thing called "husband"? Have you no heart to feel, no mind to think, no reason to judge, no will to act? Through your marriage you acquired a brilliant condition: luxury, glory, and honor. Death robbed you all at once of your husband and your protector—you became a widow both at heart and in condition. Death came and carried off the honors you enjoyed, leaving you with a child and the heavy responsibility of protecting your immaculate name. In reaction, you change your role to become a victim and a spectator. You transform your lifestyle, you become depressed. Your depression is not the expression of great sorrow. It is, instead, the expression of being deprived of a protective marriage which formed your strength and beneath which any missteps would be hidden no matter what the cost. So did you need a guide to learn how to act and to remain within the bounds of propriety? And when that guide disappeared are you then incapable of carrying on? If that is the case, you were acting under the influence of another, not that of your own innate love of honor or duty. Whoever gathers strength from without and not from within is always in a precarious position. The weak strength that is in us is better than the great which springs from others.

The former is a power influenced by the extent of our own vigor and action, a power whose persistent realization depends upon our individual lives.

You used to live a comparatively free life, under the shadow of a protector, and now you are oppressed—you neither speak, nor act, openly. Do you know why? It is because until today you did not have the independent initiative to decide on a single circumstance. Instead, you followed the path of convention and prejudice. Today, when the carriage of fortune has thrown you to the ground, you find yourself in a different world. Whatever you had been, you had been because of your husband. And what are you today, relying solely on your own strength? You always thought and acted in accordance with the received rules and the tastes of others. Did you ever venture against public opinion when you did something proper or even something good? Did you ever have the bravery to feel what your heart wanted to feel, to think what your mind wanted to think, or to judge as your common sense wanted to judge? No, you never possessed that bravery. Your husband was your guide, and the world of prejudice was your school. Deprived of your protector, you are now abandoned to tribulations, envy, and deception. I understand your fear as you resist the three-headed monster of public opinion, beneath which falsehoods and insincerities find cover. I understand your timidity in speaking and acting because you have only womanly love of honor to defend yourself. You never appealed to it for protection because you thought it weak. But this love of honor is for us the only source of strength and the only sure thing.

Listen to me. The truth is sometimes sullied by the dirt of accusations. But, in the end, by brushing those specks away, the truth emerges, brilliant once more. Purity is never a matter of enduring slander. Slander is heaped on whatever hides immorality behind a beautiful facade. Falsehood can never shine with the true colors of the beautiful. It can only be painted with something whose colors will immediately run when put to the test.

You will not convince me that you are an elevated woman by hiding in the refuge of your home, nor by publicly obeying the rules of society—it is often the case that crimes are committed in private, and darkness conceals many missteps. I would rather see you on the stage of this world, where all would see you wrestling against the storms and overcoming them. Wherever there is no battle, there is no victory. The courage of the soldier is revealed on the battlefield. Leave, then, the solitude that has buried you and reveal to this world that a free woman—free in her actions and ideas—has the right to respect as well as self-worth, especially if she herself demands that respect. Keep the good and just customs and laws of society for yourself, stamp out anything that debases you, see the prejudices that have progressed for centuries with daring eyes, examine them from all points of view, familiarize yourself with them, and then you will notice those colossal proportions diminish and, instead of a terrible monster, you will see a dwarf that you can scornfully reject. Prejudice is injustice, injustice is falsehood. To lie is to spit upon the face of truth.

Woman is the sacrifice of prejudice and society—a sacrifice adorned with flowers and perfumed with as much incense as her master's strength allows. But when her master falls, she falls along with him, and when he dies, all her hopes are extinguished. Then members of society strip the woman of her ornaments and, abandoning her to powerlessness, they loudly exclaim, "Because you are a woman, the doors of greatness and honor to which knowledge and merit lead are closed to you." Thinking that they are doing us a favor, they leave us to live life alone without even considering our livelihoods. And all those who previously would have begged for a single glance from you when you had a powerful husband now hardly acknowledge you. And yet the woman who was a queen only yesterday and is today a miserable and wretched being still seeks to appease an unjust and unmerciful society which is always ready to put her to death with its catastrophic verdicts, without considering her suffering, her tears, her sleeplessness, her desertion, and all the heroic efforts through which she strives against misfortune with thoughts of securing her life.

Mayda, you complain about the injustice of society. But what does it matter to you when you have a heart for loving, a mind for thinking, and a will for acting? You are free—act! Whoever is free and acts cannot succumb to pity. You are the owner of your actions and your fortune. You are devoted to yourself now and not a shadow. You are a voice and not an echo. You are the dawn that brings good tidings—no, you are not to be pitied.

———◦◆◦———

Mayda to Mme Sira

Give me a moment to collect myself! Let me recover! Who could possibly measure my misfortunes? I have buried my past happy days in the grave. Now I am the sad present that carries pain and depression in its hands. In vain do I close my eyes. Everywhere I feel the cold reality. I feel their rigid blinks. In vain do I wish to flee from my gloomy fortune. Oh! I encounter it everywhere.

———◦◆◦———

Mme Sira to Mayda

What ends are served by your constant grumbling? Pain consumes the soul—it hollows out the soul bit by bit and destroys it in the end. You attenuate your soul by crying about the past. To plant a tree right now in order to harvest its fruits in the future—this is the kind of conduct worthy of a rational being who recognizes her calling on this earth. You lament a greatness that had been based on your husband's brilliance. You cry because you have gained nothing in property, of which you too deserved a portion. You had appropriated the fruits of someone else's labor to such an extent that you seemed to be their rightful owner, and you lament that loss today as if you had acquired that bounty by the sweat of your own brow. Remember—only that which springs from us and lives through us is long-lasting.

You want honor and respect? Earn them yourself. You are a mother, and so you have the responsibility of raising a future wife and mother. Your mind is experienced and enlightened—use it in the service of humankind! Attack the darkness beneath which falsehoods and injustice conceal themselves! The malicious stand haughtily while society walks about hunched over. The clanging of weapons stifles the cries of the oppressed, the debaucheries of the oppressor, and the wails of the pillaged. The master and the slave, the persecutor and the persecuted, the rich and the poor—they go ahead rubbing shoulders with each other, striking one another, blending cries of joy and suffering. Some trample, others are trampled. Here is a vast field for you to cultivate, Mayda. In seeing general misery, you will forget your own. When facing general injustice, forget that you too are subject to it. Stifle your wails in the quiet wails of society. Wipe your tears, stand tall, and get going.

And if those who pretend not to recognize you or are surprised at seeing you standing tall when they thought you destroyed ask, "Where are you going?" respond, "You condemned me to darkness and loss, and now I stand on my feet. You brought forth your prejudices in front of me, and now I trample upon them and pass, for I can move on by myself."

14

Join the friends of justice, join those who promise truth and arms for the work. The honors you will gain in this arena will live as long as you do, and even after your death. Working for a great principle is acting for the sake of eternity; you will not mourn the loss of your transient greatness as you do now. So cast aside your sorrow, which frustrates your drive to action. Look around you and observe how, from the lowly worm to the fiery worlds above our heads, everything exhibits change and vitality, and submits to the highest law, that is, the law of change. When taking all individual parts as a whole, we can see that humanity's balance is maintained through many individual actions—what right have you to leave unfinished that portion that has been allotted to you? Since when has the sky ceased bathing us in its light, nature ceased bearing fruit, the birds' singing, the brook's babbling, the flower spreading its fragrance, and everything bounded by the world of harmony?

Is it only people who have the right to deviate from the universal law and abandon whatever calling they have for fecundity and life? The afflicted life acclimates people to laziness, frustrates their creative and active powers, hinders their flight, and condemns them to crawling. Intense pain parallels great success. Both lead us astray. The first leads to a loss of sensation, the second to a loss of care. I repeat, Mayda—put an end to your anguish. Your past has already plunged into the rushing waters of oblivion. You are seeking its traces in vain in a present that terrifies and menaces you. The past pampered you as a dear, tender child. The present will make a woman out of you in the face of misfortune, giving courage to your soul. It will force you to appeal to the treasures of your thoughts and your heart. It will train you to venture against danger and to look at life with untroubled and fearless eyes. Perhaps the woman is not worthy of the child? The first embodies strength, the second, grace.

Mayda to Mme Sira

Do not condemn me so quickly! You do not know how many afflictions burden my heart. Who could possibly see its depths and comprehend the weight beneath which it groans? The changes to my condition surprise me so much that I doubt whether I am awake or dreaming. What a fall, what depression—poor heart, no one knows how much you silently groan!

Mme Sira to Mayda

The human heart is a furnace wherein human history is forged. Who perceives its bottom and who could possibly descend that far? Can you account for all the beatings of the heart? Each heartbeat is the product of tears that are a soul's ethereal fragments or a smile that, like a spring flower, beautifies life's environs. It is the product of a glimmer of love that is the heart's dawn, or a moan of deceit that is a monster who carries a black grave above its head. Each teardrop, each smile, each glimmer of love, each moan of deceit—each contains one part of the story of life. Why complain if outsiders cannot comprehend the entirety of that story? But first tell me, do you yourself perceive all of that? Did you count all the resplendent traces that joy has left in your heart? Did you notice the ruin of the flower of hope that you plucked and later buried in the grave of your heart, lamenting, "One more piece of decay . . . great, one less relic of life"? Did you count all of your dreams of happiness and how many times you raised your eyes to perhaps find there whatever you were missing? Did you count how many tears flowed from your eyes? Tell me, did you count all of these things? Of course you didn't! You are ignorant of those numbers and in vain would you ever know them. Each heartbeat of sorrow is destroyed in the ignoble void of the heart, while the one that follows seems like its sad continuation. You can only mark the flashes of joy. But hardly do you begin to count them off when a bitter teardrop washes away even its memory. No, you yourself do not perceive the elation, sadness, and desires of your heart.

Tell me, do you know what you want? It seems that you do, but you are so very mistaken. You always want the impossible. Even when you fulfill your goal, you roll your eyes with indifference. You set your sights on new goals that are only as good as how difficult they are to attain. You view these goals at a distance because their immense dimensions are lost when seen up close.

Life is a necklace whose links are formed from our desires. As those desires are realized, new ones emerge. In the end, death breaks that chain necklace into pieces before we have reached the final link. Clip the wings of your desires and limit them to the realm of your duties. Choose your purpose to match the calling of a rational being on this earth and pursue it. Constantly strive to push forward or perfect that branch of work you have chosen. Scorn any obstacles, for endurance overcomes them; there is no ailment whose cure cannot be found when you have decisive will. Choose reality as your purpose. Keep unclear wishes and your attraction to the far-fetched for those times when you are tired of life's harsh realities and you want to be momentarily enlivened once more, immersed in the sweet pleasures of the imagination. The fewer your desires and sweet fantasies, the freer you will be of delusion.

Are ten bits of joy worth one delusion? Joyous fantasies and pleasures enliven and beautify life with enchanting promises.

But the delusions of the heart are the furies of hell who hiss around people, tear off bloody chunks of flesh, and throw them into the face of society that laughs, condemns, and rejoices. Wretched humankind! You mock tears, cries, and drops of blood still warm with the fire of the heart from which they sprang. And that laughter directed toward a neighbor gradually grows into the laugh of a monster that cruelly oppresses a deserted victim—that is, a heart full of life. And that shattered heart, whose beats attenuate bit by bit, finally exhales its last sorrowful breath, remaining eternally motionless. The earth is opened, the earth is shut, covering the ardent heart with the bitter cold of death. The indifferent glance of the passer-by does not perceive the hole which contains a grand story. They don't notice the story of a heart that dreamed, loved, suffered, and cried, a heart that was abandoned, condemned, and against which a prejudiced society acted as executioner when what that poor heart needed was a merciful hand to tend its bitter wounds.

Everything is conditional in society. There is no mercy if someone dares to act or to love in opposition to its laws and prescriptions. For instance, religion—which is the consolation of the soul—can be transformed into fanaticism and even hatred. And love—which is the sustenance of the heart—can be transformed into destruction and even treachery. And so, if we ever encounter a spotless heart that still nurtures that beautiful feeling, no one believes it. These wretched hearts are assumed to be illusions and are torn to pieces by derisive laughter.

Avarice almost always takes shelter behind love and faith. The smile, like the prayer, covers a trap. People reveal themselves only partially so as not to betray their true intentions. They display someone else while secretly fulfilling their own interests. The darkness has grown so thick that no one believes the light. And, if it suddenly shines, our eyes are blinded and we once again seek the darkness for relief. We doubt everything, even the truth. Falsehood has occupied the place of truth; the ugly, that of the beautiful; vice, of virtue. In order not to be disloyal to society, we turn into liars for ourselves, our conscience, our hearts, and our upbringing. Emboldened by that lie, we assuredly say, "Such is life."

But you, Mayda, raise yourself higher than falsehood and gain. Be as great as justice, great as truth, great as sacred love. Avoid darkness, avoid falsehood. Do not fear being left alone, for there will always be a few singular minds to join you, both from afar and nearby. And what does it matter to you that you are left alone? Your soul gathers strength from within, in the love of justice and truth. That which is truly great does not need another—it is the weak who need constant support.

Mayda to Mme Sira

I was oppressed by the burden of my depression and the new responsibility fated by my condition. I was aimlessly floating in the abyss of despair when your redeeming voice urged me to get up, take courage, and ensure my daughter's steps in the treacherous road of life.

Though only a short while ago I was being led, it is now necessary to stand as a leader without any guiding experience. I have entered into a new world whose paths confound me. And each mistake I make could be costly, of course. My responsibility terrifies me, and yet I will take it upon myself because I am both mother and father at once. My material means are limited (though my husband's financial undertakings could have secured a bright future for me if they had not come across such adversity that perhaps even hastened his death). The name I bear is honorable and my responsibility is infinite. I am not ashamed to fall down the social ladder and I am ready to work—if need be—and even to take pride in my work. I understand that my former success hid the rough road of life; my present misfortune reveals that road clearly. I was frightened at first, but after the initial unsavory effects ran their course, I realized that people can grow accustomed to anything, even things that seemed impossible before.

You already know well that the days of my childhood floated by in happiness. My mother was an angel of selflessness. She sacrificed herself for my father and me. My father used to worship me as I was his only child. With his modest wealth, he wished to provide me with all the pleasures of life, and that fatherly weakness could have been perhaps catastrophic for me if my mother's justified strictness had not kept me in check. Mr. Teodossian saw me and took a liking. I married him when I was fifteen and he was forty. He was rich and enjoyed much honor. I relished what high social standing and wealth could afford, as well as the treasures that spring from a noble heart. After my parents completed their duty, I suppose they found it unnecessary to live any longer. My mother was the first to leave me an orphan and my father followed her example. That double loss left me inconsolable, and I do not know how my depression would have found relief had I been deprived of the affection of my husband as well as the cuddles and graceful smiles of my baby girl, who was born a year after my marriage. Time provided the remedy for my pains and, obeying my husband's desires, I returned to worldly pleasures I had renounced for some time. You already know what kind of successes my youth and upbringing had prepared for me in various circles. You also know in what kind of luxury I lived. My husband died, and my success and peace died with him. Everything was lost, I have only ruins surrounding me along with the sad memory of my glorious past.

Now I have withdrawn to an obscure village on the Asian shore. Hissar[1] is blessed by natural beauty. Verdant hilltops form a crown upon its head and the various colors of the houses blend with the blue of the sea in a stunning competition. It is as if the Bosphorus purposefully gathered its waters through the narrows so that Hissar-in-Asia is brought closer to its sister, Hissar-in-Europe. The latter bursts of melancholic beauty with its mournful cypresses that watch unceasingly over those tombs where the babbling waters lull the dead to sleep with their murmurs—wavy forts that seem to defend against the violations of daring hands. Hissar-in-Asia is not deprived of historical advantages either. It is verified that the Persian king Darius passed his army through here during his campaign against the Scythians, who were assembled in the Danubian provinces and who, in taking flight, yet always marching ahead, forced the haughty king to fall back, taking the shameful memory of that retreat with him.

You already know of the magnificent houses of Hissar and their vast gardens. For a fair price, I bought a house by the shore which used to be a pleasure den for a rich Turk. An enchantingly beautiful young Circassian woman had been brought there for him, and he loved her with infinite passion. This beauty's early death transformed the house into a sorrowful monument to love that its owner could no longer bear. Not only had he pledged never to return to that place, he also excluded the gloomy dwelling from his inheritance. As with almost all big buildings inhabited by Turks, the house is comprised of two parts—that is, the women's quarters and the men's quarters. I claimed the women's quarters for myself because it is not as large as the other part, The two quarters are separated from one another by a traditional and advantageous feature of Turkish dwellings—a beautiful embankment that spreads across the length of my house. I walk around there every night, pondering my past and my future.[2]

My life passes by, sad and silent. I occupy myself with the upbringing of my Houlianée, which is my most important work and my only consolation. I have resolved to teach my daughter the vicissitudes of life. I want her to experience as much as possible, to be ready to encounter all those unfortunate events that unexpectedly besieged me, so that she too not find herself one day unprepared before the unknown. This is what happened to me when I was left to my own devices. Broken-hearted, I saw myself at the mercy of a dreadful dream or the plaything of fortune. When my condition began to improve somewhat, my anxieties intensified, and I felt my desertion, my powerlessness, and my ignorance in affairs all the more deeply. It is in such circumstances that the inexperienced woman, fumbling from mistake to mistake, approaches loss and crowns her labors with catastrophe for herself and her family. If a merciful heart were to ease a woman's first steps in the arena of life, that woman would be blessed. Blessed, too, is the woman whose delicate feet withstand the blows and hold her upright to the end.

It is difficult for me to understand this injustice of humankind regarding women which, by removing women from the affairs of work, leaves single women alone in the end as the masters. I do not comprehend why, in that case, society places family interests—the management of which demands knowledge of those affairs—into our hands. How could it hand over to women a responsibility whose heights they do not reach? What follows from this conduct? The woman, taking her powerlessness into consideration, entrusts the management of her affairs to the hands of strangers, and those caretakers abuse that trust for their own gain. Thus, the woman accustomed to luxury is suddenly abandoned to poverty along with her children.

This explains, then, that I owe my difficult state of affairs to social convention. I must learn the affairs of work and carry out the responsibilities of mother and father all at once. And if I were to need the help of friends to manage my best interests, my forced relationships would subject me to trials whose harshness would match my utter defenselessness. But I will scorn the trials thanks to your counsels, my friend. I will find my moral strength in my love of honor and in the purity of my life.

Let telltale tongues condemn my womanly stature to silence. I am taking your advice—I want to show myself as an example to society that a woman who relies on her feeling of duty can act freely in the paths that her conscience, her mind, and her virtue spread out before her.

And so catastrophes plunge me into the deep night where roaring thunders besiege me everywhere. I shelter the fragile boat of my life as a wise captain at the helm—I will keep my boat in a safe port until the skies clear again, when my terrifying watch will pay off in safety.

My dear, you who have always appeared as a selfless mother to me, continue to lead my timid and inexperienced steps. I will never keep a secret from you. You will see everything in my heart as if looking in a mirror. When you wish to look there, it pains me to say that your eyes will meet a picture of sadness.

Mme Sira to Mayda

I do not know whether I should curse fortune which robbed life's enjoyment from you, or bless the catastrophe that reveals the hidden and beautiful state which I long noticed in you. Some people become indolent when fortune smiles on them. When fortune turns its back, they find the strength to invoke hidden attributes previously unknown. People can be shaped only by the school of misfortune. Tell me, Mayda, would you have ever believed that you, a delicate young woman, accustomed to an easy life, could suddenly become a brave soldier on the battlefield of misfortune? If anyone dared to tell you that, surely you would have taken the asserter for a fool.

If I were not forced to live on the island of Corfu due to my declining health, how I would have rejoiced to share life with you and heal your pains to some extent with my love. However, necessity forces me to live in a remote place, far from Constantinople, our native land, deprived of spoken Armenian. The language is doubly beautiful when we cease to hear its robust syllables and are far away from our people, whose slightest memory alone awakens sympathy. We can easily feel when we are near, but it is distance that allows us to paint with beautiful colors what was overlooked at close range. You cannot have contempt for national feeling and simultaneously stifle it in the idea of general humankind. As much as humans love themselves, they also love whatever has a direct or indirect relationship with them, or is a part of them. They will love those who cared for them in their childhood. They will love the places where they played that remind them of the loud songs, noisy games, innocent smiles, sweet sighs of young hearts, bitter tears, dreams, and thoughts. Yes, they will always love those places that nurtured their tender bodies, they will love that first language that their mother taught them and in which they first uttered that divine word—"mother"—a charming word which sounds sweeter than all harmonies until you breathe your last. They will love those who spoke and prayed in the same language, who sang of the same forebears, the same heroes. Yes, they will love and care for their suffering brothers even if they are not proud of them. Nothing inspires as much sympathy as misfortune, and nothing has as much right to our care, work, and love. Who is more miserable than the poor and ignorant Armenian?

O you, my wretched nation, I never loved you with such great fondness as I do today, when I see you at from afar, when I am detached from you, when only the sounds of foreign tongues reach my ear, when I am unwell, when I am unable to love you with any action. You have no need of words, for they inundate you with too many already. You need only action, that is what you are missing. I have only an ineffective love to offer you, too. What is the point of my saying "I love you"? Perhaps you will hear only words, and not the feelings behind them. Let all be lost— only my nation and you, Mayda, remain for me. However, I am useless to both of you. This life of mine is superfluous. It was my lot to live distant from my own people. But I am not despondent. It only pains me. I am patient, and I never withhold that little bit that I can do as a patriot and an individual.

This island, which the heavens have endowed with the particular beauty of orange and olive orchards, where a fragrant breeze constantly blows, seems to be a jewel that stands majestically without wavering above the Greek waters. My life here has become tied to nature. I tried to find a few intelligent people to possibly form an intimate circle, but I did not succeed, a failure that condemns me to an almost solitary life. I embrace social relations as long as they do not require me to demean myself intellectually in order to be understood by others. Harmony or discord may spring from those relations and lead to the rise of similar or opposing ideas. Generally, wisdom preached by people is not the result of their convictions, but of chance, interests, or the day's ruling party and principle. It is then easy to notice frivolous and contradictory phrases of wisdom and reflections in their speech—the natural consequence of ideas that do not have firm foundations.

And coming to our sex: gossip or materialistic matters are the main subjects of conversation. Many women loudly condemn what they secretly wish to carry out or already do. They tear each other apart, they engage in covert competition, and this spirit of opposition underlies their social weakness. It intensifies a bitter state of affairs oppressed under the threefold influence of the law, religion, and prejudice. The main enemy of women is the woman herself, for she always lies in ambush like a spy with the intention of divulging the secrets of an innocent or guilty heart and cruelly deriding the plaintive dramas of others. If women protected their rights and stood in unity like a dam against the currents of prejudice and injustice that take them for sacrificed playthings and draw them away, then, having formed a powerful force of resistance, they would throw off abuses and weaken falsehood and insincerity—the two evil offspring of bondage. But women are ignorant of their interests and in their disunity provide new weapons against themselves.

And when it comes to materialistic matters, I understand that jewelry is essential for women, something none would scorn because it is a most important instrument to highlight natural attributes or to disguise physical defects. Consequently, in that way the woman perfects or corrects the handiwork of nature according to her taste regarding the ideal standards of beauty.

A beautiful woman is a masterpiece of nature. She is the magnetic point toward which eyes and hearts are drawn. She is the ideal of which men dream. She is the reality that has within her a ray, a fragrance, a smile—all of that which attracts and bewitches. She is a power in herself, or should I say that she is a painting of nature itself with all of its hearty murmurs, tender warbling, tempests, calms, light, shade, and movement. All finery, as with ornaments of beautiful taste, provides the costly frames of that large living painting. However, that painting loses its luster and worth when its frame is overbearing—such abuse diminishes the value of the painting. And so, the ornament that was meant to improve the woman actually serves to debase her with its abuse. Unfortunately, our sex has not yet understood this matter.

You do not blame me, of course, Mayda, if I voluntarily live a solitary life. I prefer my solitude over unpleasant and unbearable society, though this is not a natural condition and is not to my taste. Yes, I prefer my personal circle and favorite authors whose ideas nourish me. I live with my own thoughts, I turn them around everywhere, I examine, I investigate. This useful monotony is more pleasant to me than a variety of insignificant and insipid conversations. Although it is true that the mind is sharpened and enlivened by the collision of ideas, however, if I cannot cause it to improve at all, at least I will not diminish it through proximity with anemic minds.

Writing to you is truly a boon for me. If I cannot see you in person, at least I will have a spiritual relationship with you. It is wonderful for me to guide you from afar since I cannot do so nearby. I will watch your first steps in that new arena you have now entered. I will try to mark the tremendous rocks that will hurt your feet. Beware of verbose friendships. Too many words reveal a poverty of feelings and ideas. When the heart acts, it brings feeling into being. When the mind is occupied, it brings meaning.

You are a young woman endowed with beauty. Remove the useless from yourself, love only the good and the true, befriend them always without being influenced by prejudice. Do not be surprised if I speak to you again and again about prejudice. It is the deep wound where the vital strength of society is lost, to the misery of humankind.

Mayda to Mme Sira

The days and months have passed by. Two years have passed since I joined the army of life's workers. I found my strength, vigor, and determination in my principle of duty and in religion.

I devoted my time to form the mind and heart of my Houlianée without making her conceited, or timid. I wanted to raise her to be more or less her own leader. I hope that time will complete what I merely outlined. A few poor Armenian girls also took part in this charge of mine—I taught them our spoken Armenian language and also our national history. I encouraged their love of the Armenian nation through the stories of our old fateful glorious days, for we can only really love what is recognized and valued. I tried in particular to make them understand their responsibility on this earth as women and as mothers. With this very small act of mine, I offer my humble contribution to society.

The favorable arrangement of my activities, which I owe to a friend, secures a modest situation for me that I would perhaps have disparaged in times past, but which now seems to me filled with peace. My only friendship is with the sea, which I love immeasurably. It speaks to my mind, it agitates my heart. It also seems to swell with ardent passions, tumbling wildly and silently. And when it indolently pushes its waters forward with an almost imperceptive movement, doesn't it present the image of the afflicted soul, destined to suffer, that rests for a moment from the tempests and troubles it bears? Oh, the pain-stricken being who is resigned to living with affected calm—it is nothing more than a soul that caresses its heavy chains and smiles when hearing their clamor. What a caress and what a smile! I find in the alternating fury and calmness of the sea a surprising resemblance to the affairs of my heart. When my daughter sleeps and the friendly moon looks at me from up above, when the sky is adorned with stars and I walk around on my embankment, alone, facing eternity, many times have I felt a warm tear fall from the cold-stricken bosom of the ocean. Only my soul—and God, who had seen its downfall—could perceive the bitterness contained in those tears.

Solitude is unbearable for a heart that beats with the full force of life. Often have I thought of you, my dear, many times would my eyes, fixed upon the sea, smile at your sweet image. Often did my lips softly utter your name. Often did it seem to me that I was seeing three beloved shadows, hand in hand, gliding before me, sorrowfully looking at me. And afflicted, I would exclaim: O you, my father, mother, husband! How many times did I want to throw myself into the sea, to sink, to be lost, and to cease living…? O my God, forgive these sinful suicidal desires! O my unfortunate daughter, are your love and my boundless feelings for you not enough to make me feel fortunate?

In vain do we instruct the soul, train it, force it to submit to our will, and push it forward as an armed soldier. There are moments when it resists, twists, unties knots, torments itself, and collapses in the end, exhausted, with cries of oppression.

Perhaps these sorrow-stricken lines of mine conjure up sad ideas in you of the incomplete and incapable fulfillment of my duties, my friend. However, the soul is sometimes so burdened that, were it not to overflow occasionally, it would explode with a terrible and definitive blast. Permit my heart, then, to spill its superfluous burden on you. When it is somewhat relieved, it will once again stand on its feet and move ahead.

Mayda to Mme Sira

Not having received a reply, I write to you once again. My sighs of despair or the ray of hope should find a sad echo or glimmer in your soul. Of course I saddened you with my penultimate letter and now I will wipe away all traces of pain. It has been two weeks since an Armenian family, Torkomaduni by name, began residing in the other quarters of my house. This family is comprised of an aged woman and two male children, the first of whom has a weak frame. The family settled in this village due to the salubrious air of the Asian shore. The first son has a wife of enchanting but haughty beauty, which caused amazement in me, but not sympathy. The other son is unmarried.

You already know how easily friendships are formed in villages where the heavy and tiresome propriety of the city is unnecessary, even more so when two families who already know each other by reputation reside in nearly the same house. Since the day this family settled, we almost always visit with each other. Their luxury reminds me of my former splendor, and their abundance seems to mitigate my moderate conditions. The mother seems filled with pity for me, for I saw her secretly wipe away a tear when looking at my Houlianée—a heart that appears as an angel of love for a forlorn orphan. The two sons treat me with affectionate respect while the daughter-in-law treats me with great indifference. I can imagine a contented smile upon your lips, my dear, when you read of that aged woman's fondness for me and my daughter.

⎯⎯◈⎯⎯

Mme Sira to Mayda

You do not know the disquiet that consumed me when I thought that the long-standing illness of my heart would weigh even more heavily on your despair by robbing you of your last friend. In this deteriorating condition of mine, you communicated a piece of news that comforted me immensely. I refer to the courtesy of your new neighbors. You were right in thinking that your painful cry would cause me anxiety. However, I will not forgive you if you conceal your state of affairs from me. When sorrow is shared between two people, it seems lighter. It takes courage to voice your sorrow, but this prevents you from drowning in it. You tried to hold it all in, but your pain boiled over and erupted. Why do you condemn yourself if the love of a child is not enough to fill your empty heart? Your child is a part of you, so she and you together comprise one person. In order to fill that void, you need something outside of yourself.

The affection of your neighbor is truly a benefit for you. And the private tear is a big sign of sympathy, for nothing is as eloquent as a sincere teardrop.

And coming to the indifference of the young woman, I am not at all surprised. You are beautiful, erudite, articulate, and elegant. Is she not right to suspect that perhaps her husband is attracted to you, when men are stolen away so quickly and when they are always at the mercy of their wayward tastes and desires for charming novelties? I would not be hurting your modesty in believing that perhaps this beautiful young woman cannot so easily compete with the state of your heart and mind, and your physical state. Generally, women have a surprising knack for identifying the person who eclipses them, looking upon her superiority with ruthless eyes. She is a powerful enemy who flatters in public and undermines in private. You see, then, that you add positive attributes to your advantageous novelty that may make you appear dangerous in the eyes of the young woman who is still not sufficiently acquainted with you and consequently cannot comprehend the greatness and kindness of your heart. When she sees the angel hidden in you, then will she be forced to admit that your superiority does not cause her any trouble at all—not to her family, not in any circles—because you live removed from the world where you once appeared as a shining star.

I congratulate you on the help you have provided to your compatriot sisters—an honorable responsibility, entirely worthy of your noble soul. Try to explain life's truths to them. And if their minds do not yet understand, no matter. They will gradually become accustomed to these ideas, and one day you will see that they have borne fruit, for young minds comprehend well only what is frequently repeated to them. What use is it to hide the ugly part of life from them, only to present it later in its awful entirety? The best way is to train those delicate beings to see the ugly as well as the beautiful, and to teach them to resist the first and to love the second. The unexpected in life can be catastrophic; a single moment can determine the direction of an entire life.

I do not mean to influence your religious feelings. Keep your religion, if you find consolation there. I only fear that you might stumble into indolence by relying on an invisible power from which you seek your salvation. Human beings are meant to conquer hardships and threats and, to an extent, secure their futures and be masters over their fate. Defenseless people more acutely feel what threatens them. They prudently prepare the means to conquer these threats and gather within themselves all their strength instead of squandering it on vain hopes. When we are abandoned by the benevolent power we need, do we not become subject to the greatest depression? That desertion is either enmity or powerlessness. Many times depression ruled over you when you witnessed the dashing of your hopes, and yet did you think that your new dreams would be subject to the same fate unless you waited for the assistance of an invisible power?

⸺⬥⸺

Mayda to Mme Sira

You are mistaken, my dear, for the beautiful and holy religion does not weaken me. On the contrary, it encourages and gives hope. We are unable to comprehend divine mysteries, to follow their direction, to discern the purpose they serve. Who knows whether what we urgently request does not contain a catastrophe for us, and that the divine refusal that does away with our wish is not in fact our salvation? So allow me a religion that is a pillar as well as a source of strength during my troubles, for the idea of being abandoned to my own strength alone is enough to completely depress me. At a time when a deserted being like me looks for and finds an affectionate heart, is the sympathy of my neighbor not a sign of heavenly benevolence? Is that pity not a demonstration of heavenly love? It seems that God wanted to repay me for the losses He caused by gifting this noble woman's heart to me. I constantly bless that worthy soul who acts as a mother to us, for blessings provide the preferred perfume of a grateful heart.

And the blossoming young woman, Herika Torkomaduni, is a masterpiece of nature in her beauty. Her delicate and fair skin, blazing black eyes adorned with thick eyebrows like arched bows, the perfection of the lines of her face, her glorious height, and her other attributes would worthily meet the ideals of the finest painters. But coming to her nature, she is what I have already described: that is, very haughty and a perfect tyrant. She has made her husband her slave. He hears with his wife's ears and sees with her eyes. He is a good and harmless man who would be very lost were he not oppressed under some power. Herika is his god—to love her and to submit to her, this is his religion. And so you can easily see that this woman fears finding a dangerous enemy in me, as you assumed.

And yet, Levon, the younger of the two, is the opposite of his brother. Energetic in nature and erudite, he has an alert mind whose intelligence shines through his friendly face. It seems that he worships his mother, sympathizes with his brother, and begrudgingly tolerates his proud sister-in-law. Blessed is the woman who is meant to be his wife.

Mayda to Mme Sira

It is impossible for me to be patient. I want to communicate to you, my dear, events that invigorate me and fill me with a new happiness. So, listen to me.

For a month now, Levon's mother's cousin has arrived from Paris. We practically live in the same house. He is very knowledge-able, sparkles with natural eloquence, is lively in nature, and has a deep voice that is also melodic. So, conversing takes on a new beautiful brilliance. Beneath enlightened ideas, he is unknow-ingly a friend to slavery, that is, in regard to women. As opposed to your liberal tendencies, he wants to contain the moral life of women in a narrow circle. He tells me that to expand its limits is to be complicit in the rapid corruption of morals. In his opin-ion, to open a free field of work for women is merely spreading their delightful fragrance that should be contained under a sim-ple and modest roof. He wants to limit us to family life and to apply to us the celebrated words of Caesar, that, "Women should not be subject to the slightest suspicion." He is a despot, but an attractive despot. He loudly preaches his opinions, remaining indifferent to the influence he has, so sincere and veracious is he. His natural and noble manners have a beautiful influence on his face endowed with masculine beauty. His name is Dikran—and, believe me, he gracefully bears that noble name. How can I hide the secrets of my heart from you without remorse? Since you collected my tears, do you not have the right as well to collect the pearls of my happiness? How could you not want me to praise Providence that illuminated the darkness of my life with a glim-mer of love? I love Dikran, and as long as I have loved him, my desertion and loneliness have disappeared. I find a protector in his vigor and a father in his love. I will tell you all the details of our interactions and, in telling them, I will enjoy them once more.

Generally, we gather on our embankment at night, where Mrs. Torkomaduni frequently joins my daughter and me, sometimes Levon as well, whereas Herika and her husband barely ever. Since Dikran arrived, a member of the Torkomaduni family was added.

One night, the moon was keeping vigil in the sky, with thousands of stars surrounding it like watchful eyes, and not a single wind moved the sea, which appeared to be resting in calm. I was sitting alone on the embankment with my daughter, pondering. My noble neighbor sat down next to me, as was her habit. Dikran followed her example. We talked, but Dikran had lost his liveliness—he was sad, and his eyes, which were fixed upon me, troubled me with a silent eloquence. The melancholic beauty of the night, along with Dikran's presence and manners, moved me in such a way that it seemed an invisible hand was lifting my heart from its ruins and reviving it. I suddenly felt the moistening of my eyes and a revealing tear hanging from my eyelashes. I wanted to keep it from Dikran, who undoubtedly had already discerned my distress.

I hurriedly got up, and my fan, which had been dear to my heart because my mother had given it to me, fell into the sea. I cried out, and a second desperate cry followed the first when I saw that Dikran had dived into the sea and was victoriously returning my fan to me. My silent tears expressed my gratitude to him. Dikran, all wet, returned to the house and was followed by Mrs. Torkomaduni, who was barely recovering from the unexpected shock. And I myself entered my room, where my daughter was already in bed, beautified by the graces of innocent sleep. I tried to sleep, but in vain, for I was oppressed beneath the weight of happiness. Finally, after a useless effort, I got up, returned to my embankment, and shed many tears. Then, raising my eyes to the heavens, I kneeled and pronounced a few impassioned words plucked from eternity. It seemed as though my prayer was in harmony with the universe and that God accepted it. At that moment, I felt at one with my Creator. I wished to cease living, I was praying without interruption—when I suddenly felt a hand leaning gently on my shoulder. I raised my head and—oh!—I saw Dikran standing next to me.

"Forgive me," he said, "if I am disturbing your solitude. Having lost my urge to sleep, I got up and, while seated before my window, searching for some peace from the heavens and the sea, I suddenly saw a brilliant angelic apparition that my heart immediately recognized. Both of us have been grieving separately, but now let us join together to enjoy life, love, this beautiful night, eternity. Let us enjoy God, or it may be more correct to say that you are my god," he added, and, taking my hand into his, he kneeled.

I was trembling and, like a fool, said in a plaintive voice, "Get up! Go away! Let me go!"

"What?" he said, "You flee? Me flee? When I love you, and when for many days I have been looking for the right time to make this confession to you? I am sure you are aware of the fire devouring my soul. But I was impatient to speak about it openly and to await life or death from your lips."

Emotions kept me silent.

"Speak!" he said in a desperate voice. "Put an end to my torture!"

"Listen to me," I responded breathless, "you know that fortune has been cruel to me and has robbed me of everything, leaving only a daughter—an angel—whom it trusted to my maternal care and love. I am hers, and I must live only for her from now on."

"Fine," he said, "instead of one, we will be two to love your daughter, two to worship you. And whatever fortune snatched from you, I will return with my affection. Only say that you love me, Mayda."

A wail and one glance from me served as my answer.

"Wonderful!" he exclaimed, "I am lucky to be loved by an angel like you. I devote my life to you—let the heavens bear witness to my promise."

"Swear also," I said, "to be a selfless brother to me and to respect me as a woman, and even more so as a mother who is the keeper of her daughter's innocence."

"I swear," he responded, "to be a brother to you until the day when I will devote my life to you as a husband."

Only eternity can account for the overflowing of two souls in love, their sighs, and the beating of their hearts. We finally separated, but my heart took Dikran's image with it. I was in a stupor, aimlessly floating in the ocean of happiness like a fool. Ever since that fortunate hour, we have seen each other every night, with nature alone as witness to our love and God as confidant.

Mme Sira to Mayda

You are happy and I am happy for you. When the heart is satisfied, everything seems harmonious and dazzling. Dikran is a vast hearth that inundates you with his warmth. So enjoy your fortune and do not waste its gifts.

I, too, once had parents who adored me, a husband who pampered me, a child whom I loved with boundless love. Now I am alone, like a tree stump—adorned with leaves, looking up at the heavens—that a lightning bolt struck and ruined. I represent a past splendor and nothing else. When I loved and was loved, I did not know what life was worth, for to love is to live. Today, I resemble a spirit in the ruins singing hoarsely of past memories of glory. Woe to those who find no pleasure in the budding flower, the whistling wind, the dreaming moon, the babbling brook, the laughing child, the heart that smiles—the grand book of nature is closed to them. Their lives are merely a white sheet of paper with the word "Death" written on it. For these people, life is carrion that they process by tearing apart pieces according to their whims. When nothing remains of the corpse, they seek out the discarded parts in order to collect them and revive them with their breath—but in vain, for life can never be reborn. Did I recognize my condition in more fortunate times? After plucking the petals off the flower of happiness, I realized that nothing remained and I looked all around me in regret. I was alone and aimless.

Living without purpose is akin to emptiness. So I decided to study life dispassionately and with an objective mind. I observed that two main forces had taken over humanity—religion and injustice. Religion has turned into an instrument of oppression and torture. For instance, conscience is not free, neither is the mind, the heart, nor actions. Conscience, mind, heart, and actions comprise the free human being, and free people have been sacrificing their freedom for centuries to a class of men named the clergy—this forces people into an iron cage. In these narrow confines, people provoke one another by pushing, striking, hating, hurting, tumbling over one another in the darkness, trampling upon, and killing each other. And when light endeavors to penetrate into the depths of that black heap of humanity, it reaches only the surface, and all other parts remain plunged in darkness. That whole will be illuminated when the torch of knowledge descends into the cellar of society. But that difficult task is the epic battle of night against the dawn. Alas, until that final victory is achieved, how many victims will fall into the bosom of the night? With the emergence of each new religion, there comes a new abyss among nations, a new grave for humanity.

As for injustice, everywhere I noticed the force that vanquishes justice. I examined the master and the servant. I realized that men are the rulers, and women, the slaves. Oppressed under injustice, men lower their heads, move forward, work for their masters, pay for them, and sweat for them. They groan, they sigh, at times they may get angry. Then they resist, they stand upright for a moment, and turning, they pass and go about their way.

And as for women, they have lived until now listening to the clanging of chains without ever trying to break them apart. Born slaves, they die slaves. While they are little girls, they are deceptively worshipped for their innocence. While they are spouses, the chains become even heavier. They have omnipotent masters, they are slaves. The whip of strict laws constantly cracks over their heads. Women try to mitigate that violence with their charms, to rule over their very masters through falsehood and cunning. This conduct is a consequence of violence, it is a consequence of two split equal forces that are meant to act in unison, but one finds itself forbidden and crushed. Instead of the harmony that would have stemmed from the two united forces, troubles and tempests emerge which course through the veins of society like malicious currents. The mother, who bears humanity in her womb, is deprived of power. The authority of marriage stands above her, a tyrannical power that rules over worthy reason and delicate feelings. The mother—the midwife of humanity—instead of being nurtured with light and truth, is surrounded by prejudice and darkness. Men hoard the privileges of knowledge and power for themselves. What's surprising and ironic is that men constantly try to eliminate this darkness by superimposing their own light. So, in this way, instead of progressing, at times society falls back and at times moves forward, destroying with one hand what it creates with the other. And thus, men prefer the difficult and incomplete work in order to reserve power for themselves, instead of the painless and progressive way that can be achieved by collaborating with women on an equal basis.

Society imprisons the woman at home, telling her, "Gather your moral strength in this place. Any strength and intention you have will languish here like a long death throe. Your enclosure is these four walls. Care for your children there. This is your responsibility." Truly, the responsibility of caring for people is sublime. However, does society provide the necessary means, principles, and training on which its future depends? The young married woman very often does not know her maternal duties. From her ignorance springs error; from error, vice; from vice, corruption; from corruption, weakness—that is the breakdown and the death of society. And so, the ignorance and slavery of women threatens the foundations of society.

The woman who has become a mother finally has a purpose. But, I ask, what purpose do men give to a childless or unmarried woman who does not belong to the poor classes? Either unemployment or fatal ennui will consume her, or she will waste her time with harmful fondness for luxury. Equally in both cases, society has deprived women of the support needed to join with the activities of the opposite sex, a support which would double the advance of progress.

But women are forbidden entry to every open track, every intellectual limit, every path of glory. These are the privileges that men want to keep safe for themselves.

To justify that deprivation, men point to women's ineptitude. And yet, who has succeeded in proving that ineptitude? In fact, who is capable of proving it at all? Until now a field of work for women has not opened. The requisite state for their complete intellectual and moral cultivation has not been given to them.

So people affirm ineptitude without proof, even when history testifies to the contrary, recalling the great roles that women have played every time circumstances have allowed them to do so.

Especially when considering that these women had no prepa-
ration whatsoever to play those roles—they lacked the solid
knowledge, experience, and even practical skills—it is revealed
that women are capable of intellectual development, that they
can improve and serve the principle of progress.

But it will be objected that, if women are equal to men, why
would they voluntarily subject themselves to a debased condition, why don't they destroy the yoke that oppresses them? And
I reply by asking—were the peoples of Europe who lived as slaves
for centuries any less human than the generations that followed
who overthrew oppression when they asserted their rights through
intellectual progress?

Indolence, tradition, physical force, prejudice, and ignorance
cause humans to fall into subhuman conditions from which they
are delivered only by virtue of powers that result in the procla-
mation of rights.

Already, dissident voices have been raised against the captivity
of women and in favor of their natural rights. They themselves
have begun to recognize and demand these rights. The principle
of truth can never be stifled, for it constantly sprouts, progresses,
and stands victorious atop the ruins of injustice. But the success
of the principle of truth needs the measured work of centuries.
Though each generation acts for its inheritors, on only a few
occasions have the generations gathered the fruits of their sweat
and blood.

───── ⟞◆⟝ ─────

Mayda to Mme Sira

Forgive me if I do not respond to your reflections and am silently
surprised by them. Allow me to live with my feelings and be

revived through them. Let my soul sweetly sing beneath love's shelter. I love, and if it be necessary to repeat it for an eternity, it would not be enough. Dikran and my Houlianée are two sunbeams whose center is my soul. To see them beside me, to blend my views with theirs—what fortune, O Lord! The delicate care that Dikran has shown towards me, our sweet dreams, the future fulfillment of our plans . . . these weigh too heavily on my happiness, it's as if I sink beneath their burden. Let me sincerely confess to you—sometimes, in thinking that my cup of innocent pleasures is too full, I worry that it will overflow, taking with it the drops of my heavenly pleasure. If one day Dikran ceases to love me, I wish that he would first stop the beating of my heart. But—O unlucky mother!—do I forget that I have a daughter and that it is unforgivable to even dream of such a thing?

No, no, I do not want to darken my bright days with the threat of a black future as a likely consequence of my happiness. Truly, a heart in love holds a sun within it, the brilliance of which can be obscured by even a weak cloud. You must see that love is always surrounded by clouds. But how unjust am I to complain without having a reason! Dikran's words, manners, eyes, everything reveal that he has devoted his heart to me and that he is my protector. Just lately, when Herika, as is her habit, alluded to my reduced circumstances, Dikran looked at her with enraged eyes and said, "A woman's greatest wealth is her virtue." Herika shut her mouth, casting a glance at me which, I don't know why, terrified me. Being an intensely haughty woman, she wants everyone to bow down before her and to worship her. So imagine the effect that Dikran's harsh words had on her! It is as if this woman feels a particular pleasure in hurting me. But what does it matter? Dikran's love makes everything tolerable. Is not being loved by him and loving him enough to fortify me against all storms which could threaten me?

Dikran wanted to give me a costly jewel as a token of his fidelity, but I declined. The heart is the noblest jewel next to which all the rest have a dull brilliance. Consequently, in keeping it apart, we can protect its splendor.

⌁◆⌁

Mme Sira to Mayda

Life is a dreary garden bed that is sometimes brightened by the company of delicate and well-adorned blooms. When you encounter them, enjoy them without remembering that they will wither in your hands, because a moment of perfect happiness is worth an eternity. Dikran loves you. So what more do you want? Why do you allow suspicion to grow in your heart and his? Enjoy the present without regard for your future. Trying to read the book of the future is nothing more than snuffing out the final star in life's heavens and falling into the abyss of darkness. Recognize the worth of a moment that offers you a drop of joy. What does it matter that an intense wind will wipe it out? That drop will have had a place in your life, and your heart will have taken that into account. Love, which is selflessness and the personification of the sublime and the beautiful, has become so corrupted and putrid that the heart today considers it a dishonor to proclaim it. But you, Mayda, are a noble soul, a true woman; you have the responsibility of loving and devoting yourself—do not be ashamed of loving. On the contrary, be glorified through it, for of course you feel what greatness exists in two sincere hearts that live for each other. There is the most sublime assurance in that act.

⌁◆⌁

Mayda to Mme Sira

Dikran left. Beneath joy, a tear is always hiding, and beneath trust, fatal fear. He left! My eyes seek him in vain, my heart sees only his image.

Last night, when all were asleep and only the moon kept vigil, Dikran came to see me on our embankment. He promised me everlasting fidelity with a trembling and breathless voice. Happiness was so close, and yet it fled from me. Alas, such is life! Overwhelmed by the depths of my feelings, I saw nothing—the whole universe was Dikran. The sea no longer murmured for me, the clear sky had not a single star. Dikran's voice was the most harmonious music, his glances were a heavenly torch. How sublime it was when he said to me in a low voice, "Mayda, I swear to you that neither the heavens nor the earth will ever be able to keep me apart from you." And in so saying, he placed a gold ring on my finger, adding, "Let this be the witness to my words and let it be your constant companion, for I have collected my entire soul in this. But you also, Mayda, swear that you will always love me and me only." My heart swore before my lips could. As we separated, my eyes turned to Dikran's room and there I thought I saw a woman watching us. O Lord, how terrified I was! No, no, I was not mistaken. I was certain that I saw Herika. Woe is me, I thought, shuddering. When I glanced at the room once again, I saw nothing, as if it had been a shadow that had vanished. Dikran, having noticed the changes in me, wanted to know the cause. Unable to speak, I only pointed at the window with my finger. But he, having seen nothing, could understand nothing.

"No," I desperately exclaimed, "my eyes did not fool me. I am sure it was Herika." Dikran indignantly said, "Oh, the rogue."

"What have I done to her," I added, "that she treats me like an enemy all the time?" "What did you do, you ask?" Dikran responded, "You ruled over a heart which she hoped to conquer one day. An infinite expanse of virtue and vice exists between you and her, that is, between an angel and an unfaithful woman. That wicked woman thinks nothing of the vow of fidelity she made to her husband, she thinks nothing of the sacred name of woman, she thinks nothing of the same blood that flows through her husband's and my veins. It seems that the sinful feelings she has for me have been fanned even more by my indifference. And my scorn for her has been equally intensified. When she noticed my admiration for you, she roared like a lion, for envy consumes her."

I hesitatingly wondered whether Herika would betray my love to Mrs. Torkomaduni and to my Houlianée and whether I would become unworthy of their trust through that treachery. What will my daughter think? She will think that a stranger conquered her mother's heart and she will consider that a theft. Of course not only will her delicate heart grow sad, but I will also lose the influence I have over her. She is yet so young that she cannot know the secret of my heart and forgive me. And does society forgive the beating of a mother's heart when her daughter's can also beat the same way? Society's prejudices are meaningless so long as the matter pertains to me only. But I become wary of causing any harm to my Houlianée's heart or future.

I saw Herika the next day, but her face was impenetrable. It revealed nothing to me, although she has always taken advantage of every occasion to torment me. If only my imagination had been toying with me.

<hr>

Mayda to Mme Sira

I am impatient to tell you about something that fills me with indescribable joy. Blessed be the heavens—I have betrothed my daughter to Levon. Houlianée and Levon are two hearts worthy of each other. For some time already it seemed to me that my daughter had caught Levon's attention, but I never saw anything in particular. I noticed only a wholehearted melancholy in my Houlianée—I would hear her secret sighs, and this constantly worried me. One day, when her eyes were red, seeing that she had been crying in secret, I was filled with such pain that I took her into my arms and asked her the reason for her sorrow. "My daughter," I said, "are you keeping a secret from your mother? So you don't love me. Do you have a greater friend in this world than your mother? Who can love you more than I do? Confess your sorrow to me, for I understand from your eyes that you have been crying."

She began to cry bitterly, speechless, concealing her tender head in my arms. "Do you love Levon, my beautiful daughter?" I said, "and are you being silently consumed in this way?" "O mother!" she responded, "if only I were dead!" I became her confidant from that day. I consoled her without, however, creating grand expectations, encouraging her to place all her hopes on God and to wait. O my dear, how the tears of a child weigh heavy on a mother's heart! I did not reveal any of these matters to you so that you would be free of worry at least about this. Fortunately, my Houlianée's sorrows were not long lasting.

One day, Mrs. Torkomaduni came for a visit and informed me that she would like to make my daughter her daughter-in-law according to her heart and to Levon's wishes. There are certain emotions that people feel but can't explain. At that moment, I did not know where I was, or what I was feeling. I gave my approval with joy and then, calling my Houlianée, I told her the good news. She wrapped her arms around my neck and began to cry. Great joy, as great sorrow, has no words. The noble Mrs. Torkomaduni was so moved by this scene that, taking my Houlianée in her arms, she fervently kissed her and demanded that she call her with the hallowed name of mother henceforth.

It is so painful that such an angel of kindness will leave very soon in order to go to a remote city to live with her youngest child, who has been ill for some time.

How can I describe the first time the two betrothed saw each other? My bashful daughter could hardly look at the face of her Levon, who was silently amazed by her. My Houlianée bore on her brow the innocence and love of sixteen springs. She has been skipping like a heavenly bird on the branches of happiness since that day, releasing such delightful chirps that can spring only from those who are ignorant of falsehood, suspicion, and corruption. For my Houlianée, the world is a beautiful and tremendous musical instrument, whose tremors release a harmonious and eternal song, that is, love.

Mme Sira to Mayda

My dear Mayda, my love for you being great, I fully participate in your rejoicing. The love of innocence is a rainbow that shines with the bright colors of truth, for there is nothing insincere and fake there. Everything is trust, faith, and hope in the virgin heart. Everything sings and smiles there, even tears. The days are cloudless, everything sparkles. It is an eternal dawn without night that smiles majestically at the enduring spring. Blessed are the young hearts who see life as a precious jewel shining with the sparkles of the sun. Blessed are they whom hope has embraced. Leave that sweet fantasy to your Houlianée, let her enjoy that brief but beautiful fantasy worth life's entire reality. Awakening arrives too soon, so leave her gilded dreams to her. Faith is life, while suspicion is a long-lasting and unmerciful death throe. Innocence is faith and experience is suspicion.

———◦◆◦———

Mayda to Mme Sira

Life is a series of contrasts. Next to a fragrant flower that gazes up at the heavens, you see another that is pale with its head bent towards the ground. You see tears next to smiles, death near life.

My Houlianée, who shines with her fresh beauty and fortune, has made friends with a sickly adolescent whom, it seems, death has chosen as a bride. She is an orphan. Her mother died during childbirth. She is a flower sprouted from the grave.

Her father, Mr. Bedros T—, provides the comforts of life to that ailing orphan. But what's the use, since Hranush is deprived of maternal affection? Her life's care was handed over to those with other interests. The poor invalid came seeking a cure in the salubrious air of Asia. Her lodgings are near ours, so we see her frequently.

Next to the nearby seashore is a field shaded by centuries-old trees. A terrible quiet rules over that vast place, broken only by the warbling of birds. A sound is occasionally heard, another responds to the first, and a musical whole is unexpectedly formed. What do the birds say, what do they want? Do they recognize sorrow and joy as we do? Do they recognize the pain of a parent's heart? Do they recognize the deceit of life? Do they lament over an absent loved one? Do they weep, do they pine after impossible desires? I tried in vain to interpret their conversation. I remained unchanged in my ignorance. That enchanting place is like a pilgrimage spot for those in love with nature, it seems. We go there frequently and pass comforting hours beneath the shade of a tree. We met the unlucky Hranush in this place as she was walking around with her melancholy woman caretaker. We were overwhelmed by infinite sympathy. Her sallow face, her languid eyes, her back bent by weakness, and her sweet and sad form made her appear as a fallen angel who wanders desperately on this earth. We looked at her with affectionate eyes, and she looked at us. She cast an especially sympathetic glance at my daughter. Perhaps the closeness in age was the cause, or perhaps she noticed a comparison that revealed her entire misfortune. Scorning false decorum, youth follows the language of the heart.

And so one day, my Houlianée approached the invalid and spoke with her. They have been inseparable ever since. Hranush attached herself to my Houlianée with all the intensity of an eager heart who feels the need to love and to be sincerely loved. She calls Houlianée "sister." And Houlianée pampers Hranush with the strength of a happy heart who suffers at the misfortune of a dear companion. That sweet being sometimes calls me "mother," and she says so in order to feel herself to be Houlianée's full sister. She would tell us of her deserted condition and the self-interested conduct of those taking care of her. For these reasons, she was forced to gather all of her feelings in her heart and to take strength from the idea of God in order to withstand the blows of fortune as well as to manage the disease consuming her. This is the simple and soul-crushing story of her life.

"I know," she says, "that the autumn will be devastating for me. I will be the dry leaf that an intense wind will blow into the precipice of oblivion." These words make us immeasurably sad. My Houlianée promises a life full of the trust of youth to the young suffering one, she offers happy days before her eyes. And when she sees her powerlessness to convince her friend, she wraps her arms around Hranush's neck in tears. For my daughter, the world is contained in the love of her betrothed, her mother, and her friend. Except for Levon's love, she would wish to share everything with Hranush.

We go for a walk almost every day along with the poor girl. And whenever Levon is free, he accompanies us. Then Hranush looks at the two betrothed with melancholic satisfaction, and sometimes a bitter smile passes across her colorless lips, for her intended is the grave. The heavens no longer have any stars for her, nor the oceans any waves. Her heart is extinguished before it could ignite with fire. We recently met her father while we were walking around. Moving toward him, Hranush said, "My father! Here is that noble-hearted woman who watches over me with such pity and here is my sister." Mr. Bedros T— offered his thanks to me so pompously that the antipathy I had toward him intensified even more. He has an insincere politeness, and even though he is still young, my first impression was that he seems old. He revealed a feigned affection for his daughter that seemed to surprise her. It is ultimately painful that the man is father to such an angel.

* * *

Mme Sira to Mayda

Your ill young woman attracted my sympathy. The world has too many victims of such a fate. Without a mother, the unfortunate child is an exile, deprived of the sun, languishing little by little. She walks by, and a cold rock appears wherever she steps on this earth. Nothing equals maternal love. A mother's love is unconditional. There is no sacrifice for her. In fact I might say that life is a series of sacrifices that she does not notice, nor even feel. She loves not in order to be rewarded, but only for the sake of love. And even if she comes across her children's ingratitude, she remains a mother, that is, she still loves, she devotes what she has—her heart and her life. The greatness of maternal feeling is in its perfect selflessness. And I consider that feeling the most true, the most sublime, and the only certain one.

The mother is the earliest book of humanity. Those who do not learn how to spell with this book will always be incapable of reading the great book of nature. Such a person is blind, since the name of mother contains love's endlessness. And whosoever does not comprehend that word is deprived of the most sublime sound of creation. I do not know whether the boundlessness of maternal love often causes the ingratitude of children. Because human nature, in growing accustomed to everything, no longer feels the effect of even the greatest sacrifices. This is how one thinks to enjoy one's unique rights. But when one is deprived of those assumed rights, only then does one recognize their worth and feel the irreparable loss. An orphan is a plant from the warm climates which, being brought to a cold country, is deprived of the warmth of its bright skies. It wilts in the cold wind, it yellows, and it withers without having released its fragrance. Poor flower!

Mayda to Mme Sira

I received news from Dikran. A letter is a sublime bond of union between two loving hearts. A single word from Dikran is a reiteration of his love and fidelity. Yes, I know his heart well, and yet those repeated revelations affirm even more my faith. Why should I keep it from you? But since the sea separates us, I have moments when suspicion stands before me as a foreboding monster and presents me with a woman who separates me from Dikran. I don't know why, but terror overtakes me, making me someone who desires death. Am I not being ungrateful, however? Could a noble heart like his ever be unfaithful? Oh, my uncertainty regarding love is blasphemy! I love Dikran, he truly loves me. I know my hesitation stems from overflowing feelings.

And when they run their course, faith returns. After being the plaything of the roaring sea's waves, I return to a beautiful and pleasant shore by dreaming and worshipping.

It seems that the days of the unlucky Hranush are nearing their end. Our friendship has been indispensable for her. Consequently, when it is not possible to take a stroll with her, we keep her company at home. She constantly speaks about the dreams of her maidenly imagination which will fade away with the dream of life. "Alas," she would say, "life has never seemed so dear to me as now, when it is leaving me." Another time she murmured, "I am a wild forest that was momentarily illuminated by the brightness of lightning bolts. My life is a blank sheet upon which not a single heart wrote its name. Death alone placed its black seal there. If only you knew how catastrophic it is to renounce all of life's pleasures. I too have a soul like others, I too am young, I too knew how to love and to smile at the heavens and flowers. I came, I appeared as a sad witness to the pleasures of life, and, without participating in them, burdened with my sorrows upon my shoulders, I descend into the dark station of death, dejected."

One day her condition suddenly intensified. I sent Houlianée home and kept vigil over the invalid through the night, as a mother would her dear child. She looked at me with grateful eyes and said, "How much would I worship you were I to live! But I will watch over you from the heavens. You soothed the bitterness of my fate during these, my last days, and I bless you in return, for I have nothing else to offer except for one of the blessings of a soul in death throes." I was with her again on another day. Herika was also present. She had a surprising request. She requested my gold ring that bore Dikran's and my initials. If that poor girl knew Dikran's command that I never separate from the ring, if she knew how much of a sacrifice she was forcing me to make, of course she would not have voiced such a desire. But how could she have assumed that the ring was a pledge of love? I gave her the ring. She wore it on her finger and, kissing it, said, "It will not be separated from me until I die. Then you will once again wear it on your finger and, in this way, willingly or not, you will always remember me."

I was suddenly filled with a sense of sadness. It seemed to me that death was taking Dikran's heart away with it, and that a foreboding cloud darkened the face of my beloved and made him disappear before my eyes. I was about to let out a cry, but I came to myself, and I restrained my emotions. Hranush understood nothing, but Herika was observing me carefully at that point. What will Dikran say if he finds out that I was not obedient to his command, and especially if he finds out that his ring adorns the finger of death? He has superstitions about death. But what could I do? Would it be forgivable to deny a final desire?

Poor girl! It seems that despair tears away at her every moment. "Oh," she said, "the horizon of my life was always somber and menacing. My youth had no spring. As I was looking for flowers, I suddenly saw a pit opening beneath my feet. I looked there, I saw death smiling at me and I covered my trembling eyes." This must be what it feels like to be near death—a soul continuously tumbling through a bottomless abyss.

Mme Sira to Mayda

Human beings have moments when they dread the burden of solitude. You take care of an invalid, you keep sleepless vigil, you observe her breathing, and you think continuously that death separates you from her. You pass from emotion to emotion, you live in hesitation, you live with pain. But ultimately you live, for everything moves in you. However, when it seems that the mind is unmoved, that a person is rendered immobile by weariness, you do not know, Mayda, how bitter it is to feel solitude among the crowd, to feel that our presence does not inspire a single feeling—neither sadness nor joy, neither hope nor deceit—that we are unnoticed, that we are neither happiness nor misfortune, that our reason and feelings are destroyed, and that we are life in death. Oh, what a terrible condition!

I sometimes walk around the orange and olive groves of Corfu. When that verdant world surrounds me with its fragrant atmosphere and causes me to rejoice at its marvelous appearance, I feel like a wandering and strange spirit that silently passes by. However, there are moments when I can tell that life is awakening within me, when everything within me howls, nuzzles close, and purrs. I remember that I was a daughter, spouse, and mother. I want to form a harmony around me, whose echo would resonate in a friendly heart. But that harmony will fade away into nothingness, and not a single thing of mine will remain to awaken a memory.

I am alone in bearing the weight of my fifty years. Woe to those who have nothing to love or to hate! It is true that hatred is a terrifying companion. But in the end, emotion has an influence on us and makes us feel that we are, at the very least, alive. No, people are not made for solitude. They are links that, added to other links, serve the purpose of continuing the chain of humankind. When they remain alone, they vacillate here and there, get swept away, are persecuted, and become irrevocably lost. And so, in this way human reason and the entirety of emotions are silently pushed toward oblivion.

My personal weakness isolates me from society. In vain did we believe we could be satisfied with our thinking or works of great genius. People need dynamic reason to rejuvenate them, sometimes by glances, at other times by voices. Sighs, smiles, howls, cheerful or sad tears—these comprise life. To evade sorrow, as with pleasure, is to be destroyed, and this is my lot in this world. I am the outsider who is destined to cross her arms across her breast, waiting to be told, "Throw away life, dress it in death, in order to rest."

Mayda to Mme Sira

The curtain has been drawn, the tragedy has ended, Hranush is no more. When she came down to the garden for the last time leaning on my daughter's arm, it seemed as if autumn was being led by spring, that death had surrendered a hand to life. She rested beneath the shade of a tree and at times glancing at the sea, at the heavens, and at us, she murmured in a faint voice, "How beautiful is life, how I desire to live in order to be with you always. But I am the orphan bird who is deprived of a nest, whose wings have been broken apart, and who, when it hastens to take flight, falls to the ground releasing a cry portending death, which remains unanswered." A yellowed and dry leaf fell from a tree upon her. She took it, looked at it, and said hoarsely, "You poor little leaf, we have the same fortune. The tree of life will soon leave me prostrate as well. No bird will be sheltered by your shade, nor will any heart be supported by my heart. Unfortunate little leaf! You are my sister, for, like you, I will have a grave for my universe." These words exhausted her. We took her to her room from which she would never again emerge.

I removed my Houlianée from her dear one on the last day, wanting to spare her delicate heart. She did not think that death was so near, for youth is always nourished by hopeful dreams even when all hope is lost.

Hranush languished little by little, as if she were an angel gathering her wings for a moment in order to later take flight. But before closing her eyes forevermore, she held my hand, kissed my ring, and said, "May this be a consecration to you. Alas! I will see my Houlianée no more." She gave her words of farewell to her father, who finally appeared to be moved by this morbid scene, whereas until that very day he had revealed a cold indifference (besides the artificial affection he displayed occasionally). Unable to stop the flood of my tears before this heart-rending image, I left the room. But when I returned, Hranush was no more. I kneeled before her bed and cried bitterly. After kissing her cold hands, I wanted to take my ring, but it had been stolen from her finger. Maddened, desperate, as if I was death facing death, I entreated, I made promises to find my ring, but in vain. It had vanished without having attracted anyone's attention.

What will I say to Dikran? What explanation will I give for the loss of my ring? I told you already that he has a superstitious mind when it comes to death, and I would never disturb his peace with my confession nor cause him to think that the Sword of Damocles constantly shimmers above his head, especially when he ordered me never to be separated from the gift he gave. What explanation should I give him, my dear? Help me with your counsel! When people are intensely oppressed by pain, they don't know what to do, and they even momentarily question whether they are alive. Many times did I promise to reward the thief, affirming that I give so much importance to something that is of such little value because I consider the ring as a keepsake. But I spoke in vain, I promised in vain. O you my friend, it seems that my head will explode, for I foresee a catastrophe in my loss, as if I have a sad premonition. Oh . . .

They buried Hranush in the cemetery of a nearby village beneath a tree that she had herself chosen. We go frequently with my daughter to visit her lone grave upon which we spread beautiful and fragrant flowers. That beautiful angel does not know the fear and pain she has caused me, and yet no bitter complaint will ever disturb the peace of her grave, God forbid. I will always pray at this nearby grave with the full fervor of a soul that worships her memory.

Lately, in intense desperation, I went there alone to beg for her help. I knelt on the ground and asked her plaintively to return my ring. I imagined that she was sadly moving her head while an anguished tear flowed down her pallid face. Of course that vision was a consequence of my emotional imagination and yet, I don't know why, it is as if my mind has fixed at that exact point—losing my ability to think as well as to feel. A dreadful suspicion is consuming and killing me, and yet I must not reveal my fears to my Houlianée in order to avoid casting any gloom with my sadness on the happiness of her upcoming marriage. And there are still three months to go for the wedding. It is therefore necessary to gather all my sorrows in the depths of my soul so that not a single glance breaks through to her. Each bloody tear must be repressed and stifled, instead of providing me with relief, and weighing ever heavier upon my heart, agitates it with added torture. Blessed are those who are free to weep and to sigh. Forbidden tears are like volcanoes—how unfortunate the eruption, for a life is buried beneath its ruins.

<hr>

Mme Sira to Mayda

Have you lost your mind, Mayda? Do you want to torment yourself for no reason, to become a shadow, and to cause the funeral of your heart before it is dead?

I understand that the loss of your ring has had a sad effect on you, not because it is foreboding, but simply because it blended with the memory of a loved one. If Dikran's mind were not filled with superstition, your actions would have become much easier by telling him everything from the start. But not even the greatest geniuses have remained free from the catastrophic influence of superstition. Superstition is a monster that people have themselves created in order to battle against their reason, to be tormented, and to err by inferring good or evil from the natural course of general laws. Can't we heal prejudiced minds with the fact that the exact same events and signs have different consequences? It is a mistaken belief that the same causes in the same conditions always produce the same results.

For instance, many have lost their engagement or wedding rings, and yet that has not disrupted their happiness at all. To consider the loss of a ring to be catastrophic, it must also be assumed that, in keeping the ring safe, we would secure everlasting happiness for ourselves—can you guarantee that for those who wear rings? I admit that the person who has lost a ring is unlucky not because of that loss, but rather due to invisible and unnoticeable reasons that gave rise to unavoidable sad endings. Whatever we consider as "finished" is a continuum that reveals new things, causes them to follow one after another, produces another consequence, and assures the continuation of things. From one cause, myriads of other causes emerge—they have different effects, produce different movements, create different conclusions, and give rise to different feelings. Each person has a greater or lesser part in this general movement, and generally whatever is a part is assumed to be a whole, and whatever is a consequence, a cause.

How can a piece of metal have a prophetic quality that reveals a future catastrophe, or have some kind of surprising effect to cause events and direct them? We deny, to the point of blindness, what the simplest reflection clearly presents to us. It is as if the human mind has a tendency to wander about in aberrations and, always avoiding the light, to walk around terrified in the darkness. Without fail, people want to tie chains to their thoughts, and to torment themselves and suffer under their burden.

Returning to you, Mayda, perhaps you will argue that your loss will subject you to suspicion in the condition in which you find yourself—although I believe that your fear is superfluous. Dikran knows you well enough to be free of any suspicion. If you had revealed the circumstances to him in its whole truth, your anxieties would have ended—and I would especially urge you to carry out that confession without losing any time. But you raise the matter of Dikran's superstitions—you do not want to bring about any dark ideas. Matters can be drawn with unfavorable colors from afar, so wait for his return to tell him of the situation, relieving the colors of death as much as possible. Your presence soothes the unpleasant effects of things and, in this way, the force of the blow is mitigated.

You have become the plaything of an emotional imagination. Recover, calm down, but always act, seek, and make promises. If the reason for the theft is the love of gold, who wouldn't wish to receive more by returning the stolen object, if they are certain to remain unpunished?

Whoever has no qualms when it comes to stealing would not be ashamed of confessing to it when motivated by self-interest. Reward along with impunity and discretion would easily reveal even the most wicked thieves. So be strong! I am sure that you will once again receive the token of Dikran's love.

Herika to Bedros T—

You pine away in vain, you threaten to ruin your life in vain. I hear nothing, I believe nothing. I want proof, I demand loyalty. To love means to be the slave of the beloved, to be obedient to them, to carry out their wishes—even preposterous requests—to blindly submit and, if need be, to be ready to avenge, to stifle the voices of conscience and honor, and to battle sinfully.

But what did you do? What have you done in order to receive the rights to my heart? As if you alone burn with blazing love for me? My beauty has been devastating for many men. Was that reason enough for me to love all those people pining for me? My heart is conquered neither through sighs, nor through tears. I demand sacrifice. And whosoever is ready to be sacrificed can be assured of ruling over my soul.

Bedros T— to Herika

To worship you has become the rule of my heart, and to serve you, my only glory. Command me, then—what is the loyalty you want? Why do you speak of sacrifice? Does a heart burning with love perceive that? If you wanted my life, I would devote it to you—all you have to do is to command me. You are a queen and I am your captive. What is your will? Speak and let the greatness of the services I render equal my rewards. Listen to me, Herika. I am forty-three years old, I have enjoyed life with all the pleasures that wealth can offer. I got married when I was twenty-four. My wife was a paragon of beauty and virtue. I made her my slave and let her worship me. The cruel indifference I had toward her caused her sorrow, and I wanted to replace with luxury and

60

wealth that which I would deny as love. However, this replacement did not satisfy her. Hranush was my only child. I hoped that my wife would be able to find consolation in her maternal heart, gathering there all the intensity of her feelings. And I would be happy, for her love irritated me. But she languished day by day, and one day she went to bed for the last time. These were her final words: "Devote to your child the love that you denied me."

Hranush remained an orphan. Unfamiliar hands cared for her childhood in my house. I lived freely as a bachelor, so she never caused me any trouble.

I was young and wealthy. Many pined for me, many wished to join my social life, but not a single one of them was able to find the way to my heart. It seems that you wanted to avenge all those sighs and tears that I had caused, by setting alight an impossible passion in my heart—a passion that seems to contain some love.

When I saw you for the first time, sitting with my daughter, I was dazzled by your graceful charms and I thought that you were an angelic apparition, for I had never seen such perfection in a woman. Ever since that day, your image has been permanently stamped upon my heart, and I dreamed of nothing other than meeting you. And—glory be to my daughter for whom you had pity—I had the opportunity to see you frequently. I wished to have her sad fortune—it would have been enough to enjoy a single sympathetic glance from you.

One day, being unable to resist my torment any longer, I confessed my love to you. And you didn't even respond. I repeated the same confession and the same scornful silence was your reply. It has been some time now that you have been avoiding me and I frequent your house in vain. By depriving me of seeing you, you are killing me each day, and yet I am still alive. But if you do not put an end to your cruelty, I will put an end to my impossible sorrows—I have already told you that. Either decide upon my death or cease my torture. Tell me, what are your commands? I am ready to carry them out. Even if it be necessary to take up a murderous sword, I am ready, for my only punishment is not seeing you.

—————⋄—————

Herika to Bedros T—

You assure me that you are even ready to carry out a crime. That, however, is not my wish. I want to take revenge, but not through death, by which the torture ends, but through life, so that each day a new poison will be dispensed to the soul of my chosen victim and she will be torn to pieces by impossible pain. When you fulfill my vengeance, when I see that woman I hate plunged into the abyss of suffering and feel my heart happy at the sight of her misery, when I am no longer forced to hide my bitterness so that I strike and kill her heart, at that time will I consider you my master, submitting to your rule.

I was very young and my beauty had already caused numerous miseries. Many wanted to marry me, but my husband won the day because of his name and great wealth. His silent submission to my will and preposterous requests, along with his weakness in seeing my shortcomings with forgiveness, caused me to scorn him. I have been married for six years, and for six years my scorn has intensified day by day. Of course he loves me, but his weakness is far greater than his love, and I am sure that he would behave in the same way with any woman. What I want instead is singular sacrifice, singular love. I want to be the only one to receive that which is denied to others. I ultimately want a heart, a conduct, such as yours.

Ever since my marriage, many times did I see my husband's relative who, an orphan since his childhood, was raised alongside him beneath the family roof, receiving a superb upbringing. In the end, his intellectual abilities and cleverness allowed him to settle and open his own business in Paris. When I saw him for the first time, his noble manners, handsome appearance, and irresistible eloquence had such an effect on me that it intensified day by day. He exhibited a respectable brotherly conduct toward me and nothing else. My heart burned with an intense fire, my mind raved. Many times I wanted to reveal my feelings to him. But when the moment of confession would arrive, I would lose my ability to speak and my tongue would remain still—he caused that much deference in me. Finally, he left, and I thought that distance would heal my condition. But how wrong I was! He had become the object of my dreams, night and day, and no other image could wipe his out.

He returned a second time, and then I made my sighs quite audible. But he would not or did not want to hear them, so that I found no improvement in my situation and became consumed with despair. One day I finally found the courage to reveal to him the condition of my heart. He was cold to me, reminded me of his family ties with my husband, the gratitude he had toward him, and I know not what else. This kind of indifference was the greatest insult to my graces, when I considered my single glance as a gift. No, I would not forgive him, but I remained hopeful. But my bitterness was complete when one day I unexpectedly discovered his love for another woman. To scorn me for another! So that was the reason for his insincere virtue.

One night, when all were asleep and only I was sleeplessly keeping vigil, I suddenly sensed the creaking of Dikran's door. I got up, spied on him, and saw . . . do you know what I saw? I saw him kneeling before a woman. I also saw that he was removing a ring from her finger and replacing it with another. I thought

I would die of despair. I kept silent about what I saw, I kept their secret, I buried my pain in my heart. Only my vengefulness remained, and I swore to separate those two hearts that worship one another and who think that no one is aware of their love. That man is Dikran Kntuni and the woman, Mayda. The call to action has been sounded. Take my revenge and then come to accept my heart as your prize. Hranush did me a great service by wearing Mayda's ring, for after her death I secretly stole it.

Now go, find Dikran. Convince him that Mayda loves you and, as proof, show him the ring which is engraved with the letters he knows.

I have become well acquainted with his nature. He is envious like Othello, and he would never marry a woman whom he has reason to suspect. If he writes a letter to Mayda or if she to Dikran, I will divert the letters through Mayda's servant. Mutual silence leading them astray, they will each think themselves abandoned by the other and they will remain separated from one another.

I have now forgotten Dikran. I remember only the insult I bear, and I never forgive insults. I will finally see Mayda tortured by doubt and languished by despair. I will subject her to the intense sorrows I was subjected to. I will set in her heart the same hellish fire that consumed me. And, in bearing witness to her misfortune, I will wipe out the memory of my past pains. I will breathe freely. Finally, I will live only to love you. My love will be measured by the satisfaction of my revenge. When you are ready to leave, come so that I can repeat to you what my pen has written. If I chose you as the one to take my revenge, it is because I am fully convinced that, after Dikran, I can love only you.

Bedros T— to Herika

Every moment that passes steals a portion of my happiness. So I will hurry tomorrow to come and receive your commands and leave the following day. How horrible is the thought of being away from you! But my wish to serve you will be my only consolation. What is life without you if not a dried-up ocean which does not have even a drop of water? I repeat to you, in order to conquer your heart I care not for crime and death—I fear only your indifference.

Mayda to Mme Sira

It has been quite some time since I have received any letters from Dikran. What might his silence mean? I do not dare, no, I do not dare to think that he has already forgotten me. Dikran, unfaithful? No, no—that is blasphemy against truth and chivalry. No, he did not lie when he swore to be faithful to me. However, who can assure me that some beauty hasn't already erased my memory and that love has not ruled over his heart in the form of someone else while he endeavored to conquer that tyrannical feeling? If he became unfaithful against his will, oh, what will my condition be? Or if one day he returns the pieces of his delinquent heart to me, what will I do with them? Of course I would reject them, for an insulted love never knows how to forgive. I will not curse him, after loving him so much. But my heart, after beating intensely, will be condemned to death. An unlucky heart has no shelter.

But I rave. No, Dikran is not unfaithful. After loving with boundless love he cannot forget me so soon. He cannot expel my image and replace it with another. My mind becomes delirious, sometimes it wanders confusedly in the darkness and sometimes it returns to the light. Nothing is equal to the torments of uncertainty, for my soul simultaneously believes and doesn't believe, it notices and doesn't notice, it lives and doesn't live. It's as if a fog surrounds the mind and heart and, when we believe to have scattered the fog, it forms thickly once again. I have moments when I pinch myself in order to feel whether I am still alive and, being assured, I sense only my uncertainty. Doubt agonizes the heart. One does not know what to want—the end of this condition or its continuation? How dull and cloudy is that glimmer of hope that quivers during this torturous time!

When I marry off my daughter, I will be free, and then I will dash off to Paris. I will inconspicuously keep watch over Dikran, I will become informed and know everything. And if he is unfaithful, he will know nothing of the steps I have taken. I will die for him, if necessary, but he must not know. And, if he is faithful, I will appeal to his forgiveness for having doubted him, and I will make amends for my transgression by worshipping him even more, if that's possible. Nothing can stop me from executing my plan, for it is a matter of life and death for me.

<hr />

Mme Sira to Mayda

I urge you to go to Paris to carry out your plan. You are young, you can have rivals. Distance is the hated bridge over which enmity, doubt, fear, and envy walk. Doubt shakes even the greatest faith, and the voice of truth coming from a beloved person reassures it. The human heart breaks for no reason but it is restored in the same way. What was ice yesterday becomes fire today, and what threatened death gives life. As soon as you are free, go, Mayda, where your heart leads you.

———◇———

Mayda to Mme Sira

The days slip by, despair alone stands unmoving before me. Many times I wrote to Dikran, without receiving a single reply. I am forgotten! Has there been a mistake? To whom should I reveal my pain? Levon could save me from doubt, and yet I want to hide my condition even from him. I was hoping to be free already by this time, but my daughter's wedding has been delayed for various reasons. I hope that it will happen very soon and that a new obstacle will not emerge.

Oh, it's been four months already that Dikran has remained silent, and yet I know that he is alive and well. My soul is darker than the night sky blackened by thick clouds.

———◇———

Mme Sira to Mayda

I understand your bitter condition, but when you cannot find an immediate cure, it remains for you to be patient and not to squander your portion of courage in despair. The time nears, you say, when you will be able to go to Paris. So calm down. Do not condemn Dikran before finding out his reasons, for perhaps you would justify him. You condemn him—who is to say that he is not doing the same to you? Calm down, my dear Mayda. In time everything will be explained to you.

Mayda to Mme Sira

For a moment, my maternal pleasure makes me forget my personal concerns. My Houlianée is married, and now she has a responsibility. In her white wedding dress, my daughter looked like an angel descended from heaven who took shelter in the arms of a mortal. And her sweet sadness that day added a new beauty to her maidenly charms.

The wedding took place at night at Levon's house in a hall that resembled a redolent and graceful garden arrayed with myriad lights and rows of colorful, fragrant flowers. The sacrament of marriage, the wholehearted Gospel exhortations, and the accompanying church music had such an effect on me that my tears were silently flowing while I was soaring. Several feelings and thoughts besieged my heart and mind; they made me forget that I was in a crowd. But when I recovered once again, as if waking up from a dream, I saw that Herika was observing me with such fierce eyes, as if I were prey which she was preparing to mercilessly tear apart. However, this woman was splendidly adorned with pearls and diamonds, and she shone with such extraordinary elegance that she ruthlessly eclipsed all the young beauties around her. You might think that they had the responsibility of revealing the excesses of her charms.

But when she started to waltz to the music, intoxicated with the speed of the dance, she was moving so rapidly it was as if she was extending her wings. But when the final notes of music rang and when the rise and fall of her beautiful bosom was manifesting the delight she was feeling, perhaps you would assume that she was pained because of the brevity of that pleasure. When Herika dances, she seems to be a divine apparition that leads the minds and hearts of people astray. When she walks, she seems to be a despotic queen or, so much the better to say, an evil spirit that abandons people to perdition. Enchantment followed wherever she passed. She perceived her worth, certain of the profound effect she was having. There is nothing that causes as much certainty in a woman as the realization that she is beautiful, for beauty is an irresistible force which the great, the wise, the despot, everyone ultimately bows down before in adoration.

Herika is so greatly accustomed to enchanting others that she cannot bear Dikran's indifference. The more a woman is used to being worshipped, the greater the difficulty in forgiving those who ignore her. Consequently she forgives neither Dikran, nor me, for the attention he gave me.

The glances cast at me on the wedding night were so filled with infinite evil that, I don't know why, they frighten me though I make every effort to ignore them. What relationship does this woman have with my fortune? Dikran scorns her, and gives no importance at all to her words. And, finally, of what could she accuse me, even if she wanted to harm me? There are things in this world that my soul bears without being able to interpret them, and I find myself in that condition.

I am filled with joy because my Houlianée has become Levon's wife. On the other hand, I am pained that she will live under the same roof as Herika, and innocence will fraternize with evil.

If only Mrs. Torkomaduni were not obliged to live in a remote country and were here to keep watch over my innocent daughter, while I am absent, subject to the whims of fortune.

Bedros T— to Herika

I arrived in Paris and took your vengeance. I found Dikran and told him about Mayda's friendship with Hranush, her caring, even her spending a few nights under my roof, and I added that he could ask his relatives to confirm what I told him. I convinced him that that woman had caused such passion in me that I wanted to marry her, that she rejected my proposal at first by protesting with a promise she had made another, and that she finally accepted, perhaps having noticed advantages in my condition. I said that, while I was waiting to make her my wife, I saw that she was a rogue, that she was a woman without honor, and that she betrayed me just as she sacrificed you. If you want proof, I added, here is your ring that you had given to her, which she removed from her finger and handed over to me that day when she promised to always love me.

He took it, trembling. He saw the letters inside, threw it to the ground with an intense cry, and trampled upon it, exclaiming, "Let nothing remain of past memories!" in a thundering voice. "Mayda betrayed me," he said to himself. "I thought her an angel and she was a devil. I thought her truth and she was falsehood. So it seems that snakes had made a nest in her heart? If that woman knew with what infinite passion I loved her, she would regret her loss. Now all of my love has been turned into scorn, there is no more Mayda. You have died, deceitful Mayda, for Dikran!" he exclaimed with savage despair. But his despair formed my happiness, for your commands were being carried out.

"By betraying Mayda to you," I told Dikran, "I am taking revenge. That woman has to be disgraced just as she made others suffer. If she tries to approach you again, however, to convince you with her bewitching tongue, be careful, for she must find her punishment in desertion." Dikran was listening to me as if without hearing—so much pain had dulled his senses. It is clear that he was profoundly in love with Mayda.

And if that woman managed to have such a profound impact, imagine, Herika, that you with your matchless beauty, how deep and incurable a wound you have opened in my heart, a wound that your delicate fingers alone can heal.

My duty is done. I return to Constantinople. The pleasures and excitement of Paris have no effect at all on me. For me, the universe terminates at one point, that is, the point where you are found. The world has one woman alone and that is you. There is one happiness, and it is the enjoyment of your love.

<hr />

Mayda to Mme Sira

As I was making preparations to travel, I was overcome with such a fever that I was forced to stay bedridden for three weeks. Does it come as a surprise that my weak body was shaken with so many emotions, sorrows, and joys mixed with sadness? My Houlianée, with her never-ending care, comforted me with her filial love. And Herika came to visit me a few times, perhaps in order to let me know about the deteriorating condition of Dikran's affairs. She observed my face with interest, of course trying to find traces of bitterness. But her hopes were frustrated! The hand that wanted to wound was curative, the enemy was unknowingly playing the role of a friend. And Herika, of whom I had never been fond, seemed to be a revered being in my eyes. I felt some consolation in my impossible anxieties by assuming that Dikran had been keeping silent in order to keep from me the losses he had borne so as not to cause me sorrow. Levon as well confirmed Dikran's losses, although the losses were not so great in themselves, he said. But Dikran does not know perhaps that the only catastrophe for me would be the loss of his heart. I would wish the contrary, that his failure would be great so that I could demonstrate to him the disinterestedness of my feelings— to love him in poverty as I loved him in wealth—and, in devoting myself to him, I would help, console, and, rather than empty words, I would reveal my love for him in actions. Demonstrations of selflessness are never considered superfluous in love, for every time it seems the first time love is being given. And when the heart ceases to provide new proof, it is thought to have ceased loving as well.

I will leave with the first steamship to Paris, straight to meet Dikran. How slowly does time run its course! Time dashes and passes freely between happy hearts. But before the impatient and sorrowful, it crawls slowly and makes one count each movement. Happiness is a breath that is immediately exhaled. Impatience is earth that, in always giving way under one's feet, slows one's steps, while sorrow is a swamp that poisons the soil with its stench. I came to know all three of these.

<hr/>

Levon to Dikran

It is more than a month since Mayda left for Paris and we still have no news from her. Houlianée is desperate, she is inconsolable, she is ready to go to the ends of the world to find her mother. And isn't that affection warranted? Mayda is the paragon of perfection and the best among mothers. Who wouldn't be amazed at her incredibly courageous fall from the apex of heights without attempting to hide her modest condition? Condemned to an inglorious life, she sacrificed herself for her

72

daughter's upbringing, as well as for the unlucky daughters of the nation, with complete selflessness.

And could I be forgiven for being ungrateful to her for preparing Houlianée for me, when, instead of a child, I found a mature woman who knows how to think and act, and, instead of a woman, an angel who knows how to love and sacrifice herself? Houlianée is Mayda in miniature; that is, she is filled with a sense of duty, courage, and hard work. Judge, then—how could Mayda's uncertain condition not make me anxious?

So, please acquire the necessary information and immediately communicate it to me. I hope that you would carry out this responsibility with love because you too respect Mayda as I do. I fear that she may have had an unfortunate accident in a foreign land. If you find her, be a brother to her by providing help as is appropriate.

Dikran to Levon

I was away from Paris. I had gone to England on business. Having met a virtuous and well-mannered fellow Armenian there, I married her. And now I have returned and hurry to tell you this good news, certain that your fraternal heart cannot remain indifferent to this change in my condition, although your mind be besieged with emotion in the meantime.

All my efforts to get some news from Mayda have been fruitless so far. I sympathize with your Houlianée, who sheds the precious tears of an innocent soul. May her pain find relief eventually, for virtuous and loyal people are meant to have happiness as their share. Let the evil and unfaithful ones alone be condemned to torture If only I too, in getting married, could enjoy those sweet consolations that Houlianée provides for you and could wipe out altogether those traces of pain that left my heart half-dead. I don't know whether it will be reborn.

It is true that my wife seems to have all the qualities that render the married home a paradise. But what misfortune that my heart resists and scorns every favor and ability, and instead of being happy, it stubbornly floats through swells in the sea of misfortune! What an inordinate condition if I condemn to sorrow that innocent being who has become my companion in fortune!

Oh, Levon, if I could remove that black veil spread over my heart, how much would you curse that forsaken, catastrophic name which causes me to shudder until today? For the sake of our friendship, do not ever allude to my sad love story. Its memory arouses my fury and inflames even more my heart's open wounds which I believed the care of an angelic spouse would heal. I dread to think that I have perhaps taken a wrong step dictated by my despair.

———————

Mayda to Mme Sira

I suspect your uneasiness after my long silence. Using the excuses of personal weakness and the necessity of seeing doctors in Paris, I left Constantinople, leaving behind some anguish there—that is, my daughter—and taking some hope with me—the dream of seeing Dikran. I reached Paris, the capital of the civilized world, where it's easy to see the extent to which human ingenuity can be stretched. Everything here is movement and life, and it seems that everyone wants to take advantage of time, circumstances, and events. From a few things that I saw, I concluded that everything is constantly subject to movement here—the mind, the heart, and the body. People live to act, move forward, and enjoy. But in order to judge, one must examine, compare, and study; one must especially have a free mind and heart. And I had neither one, nor the other, for I was besieged with one idea alone—to accept life from Dikran's lips or to hear the verdict of death.

As soon as I reached Paris, I hurried to where Dikran was staying and to look for him. "He is away," the doorman said in such a cold manner that it seemed he wanted to delay speaking. In front of his eyes, I flashed what makes the most lazy tongues wag willingly and, placing that miraculous piece of metal in his hands, I asked him to let me know the time of Dikran's return, adding that an obligation renders his presence necessary and each delay is harmful. "Madame," he replied, softly, "Mr. Dikran went to England and got married there. I hope that he will return in a week's time with his bride." It was as if heaven with all of its fiery hosts fell upon my head and left me lifeless. The words I heard left me deprived of a sense of being.

"What's happened to you, Madame?" the doorman asked, perturbed. I managed to come to my senses and to attribute my agitation to my long journey. Finally I asked if he could confirm the accuracy of the information he gave. "What do you mean, Madame?" he replied, "Mr. Dikran has been living in this house for years. He has always respected me with his kindness and I recently received a letter from him in which he ordered me to pre-pare everything in a proper manner to welcome his bride. Here is his letter as proof, Madame"—so saying, he handed it over to me. I recognized Dikran's handwriting. There was no room for doubt, alas.

I left that house. I began to walk, not knowing where I was going, what I was doing, and what I would do. Thoughts and feelings had died in me. I suddenly felt faint. But I saw a door, entered it, and then I don't know what happened next. When I came to, I saw that I was in a beautiful room, that a woman was watching over me, and that a noble-faced man was standing a few steps away. Where was I? Who were these two people who were sympathizing with me?

"Madame," said the noble man with a tender voice, "rest assured and consider yourself at home. You should spend a few more days in silence and calm. These are the doctor's orders. So please do not think of leaving the bed. Let us know only who your relatives are, so that they may be informed and come after you." Unable to speak, I only made signs that I had none. I could barely let them know in a weak voice that I was a foreigner.

It appears that for some twenty days I lived between life and death under the protection of this honorable person and with the care of a hired woman. As I gradually recovered, I looked with love upon my benefactor as she pampered me with the affection of a mother. One day she approached me with a cheerful face, held my hand, and asked my name. "Mayda," I replied. "What a beautiful name," she said, smiling. "But you shouldn't speak just yet," she added sweetly.

Led by a skillful doctor and with the care of my protector, I was returning to life and gathering strength. Oh, if only I hadn't come to from the torpor of death, because the memory of my pain would awaken once again . . . Finally, when I was able to speak, I blessed my benefactor with my voice, as I had already blessed him with my glances. "Tell me who you are," I said, "so that I may unceasingly bless your name and your parents." "Let it suffice for you to know for now that I am Count P—. When you are perfectly recovered, I promise to converse with you more," he replied.

After some time, I managed to walk about in my room. Since hearing that catastrophic news from the doorman, I have been in my benefactor's house. Glory to that noble-hearted Count who, having noticed my youth and forsaken condition, stood as a protector, sheltering me under his roof and arranging an unused room in his vast mansion for me.

The noble and hospitable feelings among the French are so well known that there is no need to repeat this truth. A foreigner would believe they had found a second homeland in Paris—the homeland of humanity.

Despite the Count's noble conduct, I could not forget Dikran's deception, for it is impossible to wipe out immediately a memory that one has idealized and that has taken root in one's heart. The drive to suddenly uproot it becomes dangerous, for the heart too could be pulled out along with it—consequently, it could die a harsh death. Oh, the unfaithful one! He would sacrifice me for another—so *that* was the reason for his silence. Whom to trust if Dikran turned out to be unfaithful? In general, men recognize that women rise above the love of men, while for women, God is the only entity above their love. Men love the beauty of a woman, while women want to worship a soul.

Happiness died in me, and the days and nights were being reborn on its ruins. The former were sad as thick winter days, while the latter were moved by intense dreams. The light and the dark were equally indiscernible to me. If such noble treatment, for which there is no explanation, were able to heal my heart's wounds, of course mine would have already closed. But is there any remedy for deep gashes which, spreading gradually, finally cause the heart to rot? I tried to erase a memory that relentlessly restored itself. When I believed it to be far away, I would suddenly find it next to me. Love is a kind of violence—a tremendous, irresistible force. How could a weak heart emerge victorious against it? When the chains of the heart are fragile, it is easy to break them apart. But when they are heavy, as are mine, oh, one can do nothing other than resign oneself, head lowered.

I was gaining strength little by little, and the Count was giving me a new demonstration of selflessness every day. Sometimes, he would try to cheer up my room with beautiful and elegant flowers; sometimes, he would surround me with books; sometimes, with other little offerings. He would spend part of the day with me, sometimes with cheerful and sometimes with heavy conversation, in an attempt to rid me of my weariness. I spent all my energy trying to hide my pain from him, so that I would not wound his merciful heart. His face would cloud over with sadness when I uttered an unrestrained sigh or when a tear would tremble in my eye.

I would always eat alone in my room, but one day the Count requested permission to join me at the table. "What do you mean, Count?" I said, "were you waiting for permission?"

"Thank you, madame," he responded gratefully.

"Call me Mayda," I said, "that is your right."

"Perhaps my age allows me that right," the Count added, smiling. "Your age, Count, does not seem so very much to allow you such rights, rather your selflessness toward me and your infinite kindness give you those rights."

The Count had a sympathetic expression on his face, and he seemed to be barely forty or forty-five years old. It was as if sadness was sealed upon his noble face. His eyes revealed his sharp mind, his brow was wide, his hair and beard had started to gray, he was quite tall, his voice was sweet, with a melancholic smile, his politeness was noble and natural, his conversation abundant and meaningful. A natural nobility ultimately ruled over his entire person.

One day, while we were talking, he expressed his contentment at the progress my health was making, although the colors of death had not entirely vanished from my face. "Did you wish to know who I am?" the Count asked, "Do you have the courage to hear the story of my life?"

"Do you doubt it, O Count, when I listen with such joy to your stories?" I responded. "I intensely desire to become familiar with your life, but I didn't dare to express my wish," I added.

"When you find out who I am, perhaps you too will tell me the story of your life if you judge me worthy of trust, though I am certain that you are an angel," he said.

"You are completely worthy of my trust," I responded, and I wanted to be the first to speak of my sad events. He prohibited me with beautiful politeness and spoke as follows:

"My grandfather was the Count de P—, the son of respectable but modest parents. The great Napoleon bestowed nobility and the title of count upon him. He began by serving as an ordinary soldier in Napoleon's armies and bravely waged war until the celebrated battles at Austerlitz and Jena took place. He had been witness to those days when kings would flee before Napoleon, leaving their thrones undefended, and terror-stricken people would tremble before a conqueror who would campaign while seated on the wings of victory. My grandfather, stupefied by so much glory, considered the emperor a divinity. And so did France. And in the eyes of foreigners, he was divine retribution. His name would cause terror everywhere. Thrones were his playthings. He would depose kings, give and take away crowns. Blood flowed like a river, and it was as if that blood would germinate new victories.

"Nothing causes pride and intoxicates people as much as long-lasting success. One forgets oneself, wants everything, and thinks everything possible. One wants to rule over everywhere. Impediments are thought to be nothing, people are nothing, their anger—nothing. One sees nothing, nothing causes fear. One only wants, and moves forward. Whereas the people roar with a low voice in the beginning, they later rumble, they threaten, and that indignation boiling within, agitating, suddenly bursts like a volcano, showering fire and death all around.

"My intention is not to recount the history of the past hundred years, with which you are perhaps as familiar as I am, for the history of France is also the history of all nations. Rather I will recall only those events that have some relationship with my grandfather.

"He provided so many demonstrations of courage during the Battle of Bayonne that, thinking nothing of death, he ventured forth and, even though wounded, wanted to stand on his feet again. Finally he bled so abundantly from his intense wounds that he fainted on the battlefield and they thought him dead. But he did not die, rather he lived to once again serve his beloved emperor.

"The Battle of Bayonne clearly revealed to Napoleon that the anger and resistance of the people should be taken into consideration. He had much proof of this in Moscow when the Russians, not sparing their city, set it aflame. At that time, the great army of France was martyred by burning in the fires or drowning in the blood-mixed waters of the Berezina River. There were no other means left for the French except to retreat. Fire and flames intensified the confusion of the flight by surrounding the vanquished on all sides like an implacable enemy—so too did the treacherous waters that tumbled their half-consumed bodies in victory. And also the insulted people who, combining their hatred and vengefulness, were endeavoring to destroy that tyrant. He had unmercifully trampled upon them as an absolute ruler, robbing the thrones of their kings and bestowing them upon his brothers, relatives, and commanders, taking into consideration only his personal interests.

"Waging war like a lion in the devastating battle for Moscow, my grandfather provided demonstrations of extraordinary courage and such selflessness regarding the emperor that the emperor pinned the medal to his breast with his own hands, at the same rime bestowing the rank of general. My grandfather had such enthusiasm for

Napoleon that he wished to have a few lives to devote to him, and the one he did have he sacrificed to his beloved emperor on the fields of Waterloo, which became the final day of the grand drama of the empire.

"My father, an only child, inherited his father's zeal for Napoleon and vast wealth. Remaining loyal to that great figure he worshipped until the end of his life, he never pledged to serve the Bourbon dynasty, re-established in 1815, as I was never inclined to serve Napoleon III, who, with the events of December 2, officiated over his accession. The dark day of Sedan proved me perfectly right.

"France ceased to be an empire for the second time, and she was abandoned to perdition by an enemy with an unquenchable hatred who wanted to completely destroy her in order to escape from her vengefulness. Consequently, the French forgot about the diversity of their political parties and about their opposition to one another. They were of one mind for the defense of the homeland.

"I was a child of France. I offered my soul, my arm, and my purse to her. My blood was spilled for her. After driving the enemy away from the homeland due to the patriotic spirit emanating from each French heart, instead of breathing freely, France began to tear out her insides with her own hands . . . Bonapartists, Orléanists, Bourbonists, Republicans, and Socialists, would passionately strike at one another, overthrow each other, brandish their swords, and shake the sky with their thundering crashes. Blood would abundantly flow, brothers would wet their feet in the blood of their brothers, they would observe marks of blood on their breasts without any sense of foreboding, fire would spare no one, it would devour everything like a furious monster. Out of this competition, this confusion, blood, and fire, the Republic emerged. France was free.

"I stayed loyal to my family legacy, that is, to the memory of Napoleon the Great. I consider the emperor to be the outstanding figure of this and the past century—someone who stepped upon the Republic and climbed up the royal stairs. He found France in a state of anarchy. He organized her, gave her laws, took her from victory to victory, and brought her to the top of the summit, only to toss her into the ditch of misery in the end. Even those people for whom she once had contempt marched victoriously in France, led by their kings. Oppressed by foreign hands, the empire let out its cry of death, and Napoleon bid his final farewell beneath foreign oppression.

"Although Napoleon made mistakes, nevertheless he will remain great, and the era that gave birth to him will be rightfully glorified. Napoleon owes his heights to the revolution and his successes to his genius, tireless work, perspicacity, and actions. His mistakes emerged from human nature, his monstrous ambition—fueled by success—and the affairs that conspired against him. I am amazed by Napoleon; I love the Republic. Twice it came out of blood and anarchy, and twice it was ruined by two different Napoleons, the Greater and the Lesser, who stifled freedom of thought and action with their iron hands.

"Eight years have passed since that gloomy day in Sedan. I have never participated in political life. I see with pride today how the Republic is establishing itself in France. I see the revival of France strengthened with a new vital force, and progress. I become elated when I consider her appearance in the world once again as great and glorious, with her ancient hereditary abilities, after falling so low because of a weak and disgraceful government.

"The fall of France opened a tremendous hole in the civilized world. And a revived France, having a Republic instead of a crown on her head, forms the strength that stimulates enlightenment.

"The last glimmer of hope of the Napoleons languished in the grave. Consequently, the Republic has one fewer enemy and one more victory that no drop of blood can sully. The day might come when the Republic will be stifled once again—I pledge to never attend its funeral. I will not commit matricide, rather I will leave my homeland. I will flee in order not to stain my hands with her blood.

"My heart, that had been dead to every pleasure, was living for France alone when I met you, Madame.

"My father was an honorable and noble-hearted man. He had two great loves in this world—one was Napoleon, the other was his child. Aristocratic blood did not flow through my mother's veins, but what did that matter to my father, who loved her and married her? She had beauty and virtue, and that was enough for his heart. Both of them lived happily, and I was the fruit of their love. They concentrated all their cares upon me in order to make me a worthy man. I finished my education with glorious success. I was young; I worshipped my parents as much as the joys of this world. I was yet very young when I lost my father and, a short while later, my inconsolable mother. Their death drove me mad, but time relieved my sorrow and I allowed myself to enjoy life again.

"The wealthy have many friends, for all wish to associate with them. These friends endeavor to please by fulfilling their desires, flattering them, and predicting a bright future for them. Parasites stick to them, they attack from all sides, they take over their purses, they abundantly gather their gold, they create a new pleasure every day, they open a new door to lavishness until the final coin is spent, and then they turn their backs in order to seek new prey. The days and nights followed one another as did the delights of life. My wealth was subject to danger, for nothing can resist unlimited lavishness. A happy, but in the end devastating, event stopped me at the edge of the chasm, saved my purse, but made me lose my heart.

"One day, as I was taking a walk, I met a girl of enchanting beauty, as if she were one of the fair figures of Raphael who had been made incarnate by the effects of fiery love. Her manners were noble and all at once discreet. I pursued her and was informed that her father was a modest and honorable merchant. That miraculous vision left its mark on my heart. I looked for her constantly and I would follow her everywhere. She noticed me, and I was filled with joy when I observed that she was not avoiding me at all.

"One night, she was seated in front of me at the theatre. I was looking at her with wonder, my lovesick heart driven mad by the music. When the performer sang the following words, 'I can no longer silence the secret of my heart—I love you,' I jumped out of my seat as if in a delirium, looking at her. I saw that she was lowering her eyes in perturbation and that sadness surrounded her. Finally, one day, I found a way to speak with her and to reveal the flame that was devouring me and to hear her revelation of love in turn. I wanted to immediately approach her father in order to receive permission for our marriage, but, shuddering, she let me know that she was bound to be the bride of a man who worshipped her, accepting antipathy in return. Corinne would sacrifice her nineteen springs, her heart, and her gifts to her father, for any rejection would abandon her father to perdition. It was as if this bitter confession squeezed all the blood from my veins. Nevertheless I still hoped that someday that beauty would yet be mine.

"We would always see each other, worshipping one another and waiting for . . . for what? We too did not know. Finally, Corinne's betrothed wanted to proceed with the wedding ceremony, which he had found as a means to take that unlucky girl away forever. The man was threatening to completely ruin Corinne's father's merchant activities, and her father was threatening to disown his child. Frantic and desperate, I presented myself to the father of my beloved, revealed our mutual love, informed him of my willingness to make every sacrifice, and asked for his daughter as my bride.

"At first he became indignant and wanted to send me on my way. But then, seeing my tears, my youth, and hearing my urgency, he was moved to pity. He too was moved and said sympathetically, 'I sacrifice my Corinne in order to save my honor and the future of my other six children. My fortune lies in the hands of my daughter's betrothed. That man worships her and nothing would cause him to renounce my child. Tell me, what can I do? Do you think my soul does not bleed in readying my daughter's martyrdom?' How could I respond? What could I do? I wanted to elope with Corinne, but in order not to harm her father she refused—her love did not have the courage to sacrifice him.

"The day of the wedding approached, and it was as if hell with all of its fires and tortures was dwelling in me. Corinne was sad, but it appeared that she would submit to her fate. I blamed her for that reason with intense reproach, extreme bitterness, and even questioned her feelings. 'Calm down,' she would say, 'you yourself will judge whether or not I love you.'

"The day arrived that would snatch Corinne away from me forever. I had gone crazy. I wanted to abandon myself to torments by witnessing the theft of my treasure at the wedding. I went to the church a little before the time set for the ceremony. I chose a suitable place from which I could see her and be seen by her, to torture and kill her soul by displaying my fierce despair before her eyes. Countless lights were already illuminating the church, the guests were gradually arriving and taking their places, the official time for the wedding passed—and the bride and groom had not appeared. Signs of impatience began to be seen from all sides, everyone was casting their glances all around. Frenzy had taken over me; sweat was pouring from my brow. This delay was causing me joy, it was a brightness breaking through the mist of my soul, when suddenly a terrible noise rumbled through the church: 'The bride is dead!'

"At first, I was hopelessly dazed, moving neither forward, nor backward. I remained still. Then I rushed out of the church and ran to Corinne's house. A surprising contrast was in place there. Joyous wedding preparations were lost among tears and accompanying sad lamentations. Like an incensed animal I ran to Corinne's room and saw her—oh!—adorned with a white bridal gown, spread across the bed. She was resting in the sleep of death that she herself had prepared. In her crossed hands, she held that withered rose that I had given to her during our first outing, and this was the symbol of the death of our love. I threw myself on her with the desire to die with her. When I came to, I was in my own bed, with friends watching over me in my room. I had reached the gates of death; the doctors had lost all hope. Oh, why didn't their prediction come true? Then I would have been free of so much sleeplessness and despair and, although I was barely thirty years old, I would not have appeared so old in my youth, feeling indifference and disgust for life.

"Ever since that fatal day, I became a different person. My heart was dead to all pleasures and I lived only with the memory of my Corinne. I devoted my life and my wealth to relieve the miserable and especially to help unlucky lovers. The days passed by and I looked upon life as a stranger. As fate would have it, I was meant to meet you when you fainted in the store. Nobody recognized you. I stood as your protector. When your face—pale and near death— struck my eyes, I thought you were Corinne—you resembled her so much, it was amazing. The more I looked at you, the more it seemed that I could recognize the lines of her face. I had found my Corinne in you, and I was desperately trying to revive you, for I believed that losing you was like losing her one more time. Finally fortune bestowed your life to me. In your sweet glances, in your harmonious voice, your sad manners, and your melancholic smile, once again I find the treasure I had lost.

"I do not ask you who you are, Mayda, because one who looks like Corinne is of course an angel like her. I only ask whether your person and your heart are free, and, if they are, I offer myself and my heart to you."

"Alas, Count," I responded, "my person is free, but my heart is not. The turn is now yours to hear me out. It is fully your right that I make my confession to you, for you have been a brother and a father to me." I related all of my sad events, one by one, and when I finished, he got up filled with infinite outrage and said, "Would you like me to avenge you by punishing that rogue?"

"No, no," I replied, "I do not want to be a villain and shower evil on the man I once loved. Let him live and, if he has any conscience, he will be tormented by the sorrows he has caused me. And if he hasn't any, why stain your spotless hands with the vile blood of a monster?"

"That is noble of you," he said, squeezing my hands, "and I was right to think that you could only be an angel." The Count began to walk around the room in deep thought, and then he sat next to me and said, "Your wound is still very fresh. When it is healed, when some day your heart seeks a pillar, know that mine is ready for you. And if you prefer someone else over me, love him without any pangs of conscience, bestowing upon me your friendship alone. Be happy and I will be happy through you. If you leave, I will come to visit you on the shores of the Bosphorus. As long as you are here, I live through your presence and, when you are absent, with your memory. Perhaps against your wishes I will be your brother and, in my living for you, I will be living for my Corinne."

There are moments when we cannot find words to express the feelings that completely overtake us. I only extended my hand with a grateful heart to the Count. He took it silently and a teardrop fell upon it. "You will ever and always have a selfless friend in me," I said when my emotions became calm enough to allow me to speak.

"I accept it, O you noble and sublime soul," he added and left the room.

As the time neared for me to leave, I had to go out to test my endurance and acquire strength again for the journey I had to undertake. I was still weak, and as I was preparing to turn back I observed a great crowd entering a church. I entered it too, especially as my soul needed the mystical effects of a sanctuary. I observed that that holy place was adorned with particular splendor for a solemn ceremony. The crowd was large and the organ had filled the church with its majestic sound, as if it were a musical fragrance. The effects of sacred music on a sad soul are undeniable, for that music weeps, wails, and sighs. I was so overtaken by it that I was neither hearing nor seeing anything around me. I thought I had left this earth, that whatever was human had vanished from me, and I was one with God. Suddenly an unusual sound put an end to my reveries and caused me to look up. I saw before the altar a beautiful young woman who had come in a white bridal gown to join her heavenly husband, surrounded by a group of nuns whose black habits presented a contrast to the adornments of the young woman.

"Poor angel!" a noble-faced woman murmured next to me. "So young, and she already came to know the deceptions of the heart. She will bury her beauty beneath a black shroud and she will endeavor through love of religion to forget that rogue who deceived her."

That internal condition corresponded to mine. Was this a divine sign that revealed to me the course to follow? I was looking at the unfamiliar young adolescent who was a sister to me in her misery, and I was sympathizing with her and loving her. I wanted to console her, saying, "I too loved, was abandoned, and sacrificed—you are not alone."

A cheerful piece of music was being heard, beautiful voices were singing, proclaiming the bright white bride adorned with flowers. Suddenly a mournful piece of music followed the first— each note was a black sigh that burst forth from the immense sacrifice taking place. I say *immense* because nature, the heart, and youth were the ones being martyred.

The beautiful hair of that offering fell beneath merciless scissors. The joyous white clothing was replaced by ones of depressing tones, and the maiden spread her body beneath a black cover while prayers for the dead gave the sad news that a young soul was dead to the pleasures of the world, that a life of prayer and selflessness was beginning, and that the sisters of mercy had one more sister, as did the miserable ones another mother. The black covering had destroyed the woman of the world, and a virgin of the convent had burst forth from it.

This scene moved me intensely, as if I was finding some relief by this completed sacrifice. To renounce all worldly pleasures, to place an expanse between past memories and the present in order to come together in the idea of the infinite God—this was the thought that came to me with the resolve to carry it out in the future. It seemed that I felt a lightness regarding the burden of my pain, and a fierce joy filled me.

The church music had ceased and almost all the spectators had left. Silence was ruling over the holy place. My mind had been taken over by what I had seen, and my heart was content because of my thought to carry it out. I was among the last to leave the church. I got up to go, and then—oh my Lord!—I saw Dikran, arm in arm with a young woman heading for the church's door. I barely managed to stifle the cry that my heart wanted to let out. A cloud passed over my eyes and I fell once again onto the cushion. I don't know how long I remained there, faint, only that, as I was just coming to, I thought I was hearing Dikran's voice sweetly speaking to me.

I opened my eyes, but he wasn't next to me. It was only an unfamiliar man watching over me. When I could speak, I asked the man if there hadn't been someone else next to me a moment before. "No," he replied. But it was easy to suspect from his tone of voice that he was covering up the truth. I repeated my question with such urgency that the kind man was moved to pity, and he confessed that a young man had taken care of me with tears in his eyes and with affection, having left as I was coming to, commanding him not to reveal his presence there to me, while an emotional young woman by him was trying to relieve his pain. That man was the sexton of the church, and he told me that he had received a generous donation from Dikran in order to secure my necessary care. I had a carriage brought, entered it, and returned to my place, I don't know how.

The Count was consumed with great anxiety because of my lengthy absence, and he greeted me with absolute joy. But, observing that I was out of sorts, he immediately understood that I had had a strange encounter. I told him of the church ceremony and my intense incident. "Let me take your revenge at last," he said burning with outrage.

"Do you think that drops of blood heal those wounds?" I replied. "Let him live, and let his conscience be the judge."

I was preparing to part from the Count. I already loved him as a brother, and I was even prepared to devote my life to him, except for my heart. He seemed inconsolable due to my departure. "Life," he was saying, "was a burden to me. But it isn't like that now because I have a purpose, that is, to secure your future, to assure your happiness. Be happy. Whether I or someone else fulfills your future, it doesn't matter. It is enough that you be fortunate."

"O Count," I murmured between sobs, "if my heart were able to be revived beneath the ruins, it would worship you, O you most noble of men. But I fear that it has definitely died. Only know well that you have a grateful sister in me, ready at all times to be sacrificed to you and to repay you with selfless acts for all of the selfless acts you undertook."

I left Paris, and returned to the nest of my sorrows, broken-hearted and with a weak body. I found my child once again, I was consoled by her appearance, and for a moment I forgot my pains. And it was as if my Houlianée was receiving me once again from the clutches of death. Levon is like a son to me. Soon I will communicate to him my decision to withdraw from this world. During my beautiful days I had heard that there was a very proper convent in Tiflis (Tbilisi)—a shelter for souls of noble background. I wish to go there. All that remains is for Levon to take the necessary measures to have me admitted to this convent. But for now I want to enjoy my daughter's presence, to feel that I am completely a mother until I devote my life to God.

Mme Sira to Mayda

Mayda—so love blinds you to such an extent that you are willing to give up your youth, your freedom, and finally your entire life to be imprisoned within the four walls of a convent? If you wish to live afflicted, in solitude, for your God alone, if you wish to serve people in misery, should you be tied down by vows that would be impossible to break? One day you may regret what you have done. In your present desperate condition, it seems to you that time will be unable to cure your pain and that you will always remain in this sad state. Even if that were the case, is that any reason for you to cease being a mother and, condemning your daughter to orphanhood, forcing her to cry over *your living death*? But first tell me, do you even have that right? A woman who gives birth to a child vows silently to assure that child's happiness. And you, as a mother, do you want to change your Houlianée's beautiful eyes to two springs of tears? I see intense selfishness in this conduct of yours. I see that you sacrifice the one who loves you to the one who does not. Your behavior is truly unforgivable.

First, tell me if there is anything as merciless and barbarous as a convent, that nest of misery and oppression where will, emotion, and thought are chained, and where human moral sacrilege is ultimately carried out, if I am allowed to speak my mind. Can people—who are born for freedom—feel pleasure in chains? Can the heart—which has the responsibility to love—not love? Can the mind—which has no limits—be contained in the ideas of religion alone? Doesn't it reach its limits, thinking all the while that it had been serving the limitless? Everything in nature is born, freely grows, and freely lives, submitting to the general laws of the universe.

Answer me, Mayda—what will you do if one day you change your mind about your decision? That will be impossible, for they will show you the four walls of the convent. If your sorrow-stricken heart is reborn with the willingness to beat, they will show you the four walls of the convent. If your tongue, held back by grief, tries to speak someday, they will show you the four walls of the convent—that is, the gallows of thought, heart, and tongue, or so much the better to say, the death of life. So come now, give up your intention, strive, be tortured, die as necessary, but die freely. Remain a mother.

You want to be sacrificed for an ingrate who left you. In your despair do you want to give him joy by completely forgetting your dignity? Die in silence if living is not possible, but do not bestow upon that rogue the scene of your degradation. I know that love is a force that acts violently upon us and we cannot toss off its yoke even if we wanted to. I know that a love of reins and rules is no love.

I know that there is no way to extinguish the flames that burn us. However, an honorable means is left to us in this desperate competition, which is to die with grace, for a dignified death is better than a base life. And so I would like to tell you that I consider it better to lament over your great memory than to be elated by your small and miserable life. And yet, Mayda, you know that if the world offers me any pleasure, if there is a bond that ties me to life, it is your friendship. With your memory I relieve my solitude, which makes my personal incurable pains even more bitter. With your death, you would break that final link that connects me to life, you would extinguish that final glimmer which illuminates my dismal days, you would rob me of my heart's final nourishment. Nevertheless, I have the courage to cry out to you, "Die, but do not degrade yourself."

As a great favor, I ask you, Mayda: keep your freedom and carry your sorrow with courage. Look, the Count offers you his hand. Accept it, he is worthy. You are two souls meant for each another. With his fidelity, you will be able to forget the infidelity

93

of the other. You lose a monster, you find an angel. Not only do you not lose, you gain.

I do not urge you to be a companion in fortune to the Count henceforth, no. When we offer our hearts, we must give them completely or not at all. An imperfect gift is no gift, rather it is evil. And you cannot offer your whole love right now. So wait. Time will heal your disease, and the heart of the Count will hasten that healing.

I too, like you, hopelessly loved once upon a time. I thought I would die, but I lived, and I loved once again, devoting my life to a husband whom death unfortunately snatched away from me too soon. Very often I called upon death for help, but, as the memories of pain fade away, life bestows new pleasures, and then we fear losing the life we had scorned. If it were not for forgetting, what would be the state of humanity? It would be destroyed, for who can claim that they have not studied in the school of misery? So live, Mayda, for your child, for me, and for your nation.

Herika to Bedros T—

Your ingenious trick—the two letters from Dikran I seized in which he insults Mayda by mentioning her infidelity—has irreparably separated the two lovers. Of course, Mayda went to Paris to hear an explanation from Dikran. But, finding him married, she brought nothing back with her other than the shame of her defeat. She is truly pale and weak. I see that she is unhappy, for the mourning of her heart is drawn on her face. But that does not satisfy me as long as I notice a glimmer of joy in her languishing eyes and a smile of contentment across her discolored lips, as she witnesses her daughter's good fortune. I simply cannot endure even the shadow of that contentment. I want her to be unlucky as a mother as well, just as much as someone in love. I want suspicion to creep into Levon's heart so that he will be disgusted by his wife. I want tears, I want scenes of despair, so that I may strike the final blow to Mayda's heart with an unfailing hand. With each vengeance that I take, I receive new strength to live and to love you. Vengeance—a miraculous word! The life of the soul! If it weren't for vengeance, would witnessing the happiness of a hateful rival be the only sun to shine in my eyes? O terror—would I see my two sworn enemies united in love? No, no, I would prefer death a thousand times more.

You served me and I returned your services with my love. You loved me and you acted that way. Have your feelings diminished now so that you won't pledge to serve my vengeance again? Your daily pleas assure the opposite, and this last time you swore to love me always and to remain my slave always.

I will not see you for another two days. But it is impossible for me to wait that long. And so I am forced to write to you to reveal my decision. As for carrying it out, I am certain that you will manage it successfully.

We know that Houlianée has a habit of walking around the grove in the garden where Levon generally goes to greet her when he returns early from work. As soon as you realize that Levon is on his way home, immediately send an anonymous letter addressed to Houlianée in which you express pain for your absence that day, promising to make up for it on the following day. In the absence of his wife, Levon will of course read the letter and say nothing, so that he catches his wife's deceit the following day. And you, try to disguise yourself and hide out in the grove, fleeing only when you notice Levon's arrival. Act in such a way that he sees only your escape, so that he does not recognize you.

The letter, your presence, and your escape will be enough to raise Levon's suspicions because he is already suspicious in nature and surprisingly protective of his honor. He might resort to any means to avenge his insulted honor. Houlianée worships her husband and may die if deprived of his love. Then, seeing her daughter's misfortune, Mayda's soul will be filled with a new poison, she will be oppressed under a new burden, by which her life will become a long-lasting and bitter death throe. Her catastrophe is my pleasure; her tears feed my love for you.

Mayda to Mme Sira

I made my entire confession to Levon. He became intensely enraged by Dikran's conduct, especially as he had always considered him to be honorable. "If I were to judge from a few unclear lines written in his letter," he said, "perhaps he too was punished with the same treachery and is no happier than you." Levon wanted to reproach Dikran for his dishonorable behavior. But I prohibited it and he promised to remain silent.

I told him of my resolve to withdraw to a convent. He intensely opposed it, presenting several reasons to make me feel the pain Houlianée would bear. I assured him that my daughter could relieve the bitterness of her mother's absence with her love in married life, especially when it would serve my peace. "In departing, could I cease being a mother?" I asked. "Which mother could succeed in doing so?"

Against your and Levon's advice, I will carry out my design, for the weak echo of life that reaches me, the dull image of pleasures, the light movement around me, ultimately everything exacerbates and intensifies my condition. Of course the company of the unfortunate is a sad consolation for a sorrow-stricken soul. But I will find others as well who have known life's bitterness as I have, and that will perhaps give me the courage to bear my pain. I will find silence and the image of death in those four walls, as you say. And however limited life will be, my strength will be fortified such that I will be able to live out the rest of my days with greater comfort. From this world, which I renounce, I will take only the memory of my loved ones, with the condition of keeping it until my last breath. You ask me what I would do were I suddenly to be reborn from the grave and desire to love, and to think, once again. When the heart is intensely struck, it finds no salvation. There are wounds that can be healed, for they are not fatal. But those such as mine that are fatal consume life little by little, and ultimately destroy it.

You speak of marriage when I delivered my farewell address to this world. I respect and love the Count as my brother. My heart loved but once and it loved so much that it was consumed. The Count finds the loyal Corinne in me—would you have me find the deceitful Dikran in him? I wish to be resurrected again, to have another heart to offer the Count. But does wanting always mean being able?

I am already placed in the shroud of death. If I tried to toss it off, perhaps even my remaining life would be taken with it. Leave me to my lot, let me fulfill my dream. Perhaps I will find peace for a little while. And yet, would you forgive me for confessing something to you, which causes me shame? Then listen to me. There are moments when Dikran's sincere face appears before me, his words and promises echo in my ears, and at that time I feel that I could forgive him and even defend him. It seems to me that he can't stop loving me, nor I stop worshipping him. I am talking nonsense, aren't I? I would be crazy if I were to defend him and love him after his black treachery. I am a martyr, but I am sympathetic to the hand that struck a merciless blow upon my heart. I guess I hate Dikran, and yet I still worship him. It seems to me that I have forgotten him, but I always remember him.

I flee from him, and yet I always seek him. This is the impossible situation in which I constantly waver. There is an intense struggle between a reproached love and a burning heart, between my dignity and my base feelings.

⌁

The Count to Mayda

You left, Mayda, and nothingness overtook me. I lived through you briefly, and then you abandoned me to my sad fate. Darkness has surrounded me. One star shines over there, as a beacon of salvation, and that is the light of your memory. I am filled with melancholy and I feel again that life is an unbearable burden. So am I forever condemned to lose my Corinnes? Am I condemned to lament after them, after having immeasurably loved them? Tell me, Mayda, that you are not dead to me, that you will be born once again, to offer me a new heart. But is mine enough for you in return? You are so high-minded that you don't give any importance to my wealth or social standing. I know that generosity of yours. But does my selflessness suffice for you to replace that heart which you lost? Tell me, Mayda—will you love me one day? May I nurture that hope? But I don't want you to love me for the sake of pity, by sacrificing your noble heart to me. No, no, I would never approve of accepting such a burnt offering.

However, if your implacable heart cannot beat for a second time, would you at least not deny me the happiness of breathing the air that you breathe, living in the country in which you live, listening to your voice, serving you, and devoting myself to you.

It matters none to me to estrange myself from my homeland, for love is a citizen of the world. The homeland is the place where our beloved resides. I am an immigrant to my native land, and the sun of my heavens stings my eyes. A domestic affair keeps me from leaving right now. But as soon as conditions allow, I will depart from here. So, until we meet again, Mayda.

Mayda to the Count

To live for you, to compensate you for whatever I accepted from you, to cause a little happiness in your sad life—these would be the greatest of my desires. But can the black night emit light? Can a lifeless heart bestow life? And can whatever is dead live once more? I would sacrifice a few lives in order to provide you with some consolation, but alas, I have no heart to dedicate to you. The perfidious hand of fate struck my poor heart and it has remained lifeless ever since that blow. You inundated me with your kindness, and I can do nothing for you. I wish with all my heart to serve you, but I am unable to do so. To live beneath the same heavens with you, to know you as a brother, and to console you would have been my greatest wish. But my sky cannot be yours, for I will live in darkness, whereas you need light. You are beginning life, while mine is ending. I will renounce everything, I will clothe myself in death, and I will take with me only the memory of my loved ones.

Never, Count, never will I be able to forget you. When the doors of the convent close after I enter, when I recall my past days, your noble image will be one of those images to bring me pleasure. My mind will rest upon your memory like a green branch placed upon a flame, and my soul will send you from afar a song of gratitude and friendship. Be sure that, when that terrible moment arrives, I will utter your name along with the names of all my other loved ones. Farewell, Count. Why didn't fortune want me to know you first? Instead of two miserable beings, we would have been two happy ones. I hope that fortune, which has persecuted me, will not deny me a shelter in which to be buried alive. I say to you once again, farewell. Perhaps I will soon depart for a foreign land in order to fade away.

<hr />

Mayda to Mme Sira

Am I condemned every time I pick up a pen to convey the sad news of a new catastrophe? And who would have expected such an unforeseen event? Imagine that Houlianée is the target of a wicked accusation. Her eyes have become springs of tears and she no longer smiles. She fell intensely ill and I worried that I would lose her.

An anonymous letter and a man fleeing from the grove while my daughter was strolling there aroused Levon's suspicions. He who was so noble and affectionate toward his wife has seemingly turned into a fierce monster. He bitterly complained, considering himself unjustly betrayed, and he threatened to leave a house where dishonor was present, to leave Constantinople itself for good, and to go to a remote place in order to lament his misfortune. Just imagine my poor Houlianée's despair and my own! In vain did she wretchedly protest, assure him of her innocence, and with tears and sighs urge her husband to believe her innocence. When Levon was preparing to leave his married home, my daughter, unable to bear that catastrophe any longer, was overcome by such a fever that it brought her to death's door. I forgot all sorrow, all care, and lived only to save my child. During the ravings of her illness, she continuously exclaimed, "O Levon, my love! Don't leave me. I swear to you that I am innocent." Seeing his wife's desperate condition and hearing her plaintive words expressed in delirium, Levon was filled with regret and despair, and he returned with infinite love to his beloved. He bitterly lamented his previous desire to be an executioner of the innocent. "I see in such circumstances an evil spirit that wanted to disturb the happiness of my family," he said. "I will find it, and I will avenge my Houlianée."

After unbearable fears, my daughter was out of danger, and I felt what it was to become a mother for the second time. I took an oath not to be separated from her on any account, for the time being. What would my poor child do without her mother? She shed her tears on my bosom during times of despair and my words consoled her, assuring her that these are the tempests of life and that bright days would shine once more. My innocent child relied on me, hoping that I would bring Levon back to her.

When the frenzy passed and when Houlianée saw her husband by her side, it was as if she could not believe what she was seeing, and she continuously asked, "So did you believe my innocence? Do you love me again? Who could have wanted to take your heart from me? Didn't you know, then, that it is impossible for me to live without you?" Completely overcome with emotion, Levon promised to worship her and take vengeance.

It seems that this new and intense event was meant for me, so that I would forget the sorrow that consumes me. What troubles, what fear I bore! I was seeing my Houlianée accused in a cowardly manner and I was unable to prove her innocence. To be a mother and to see your child subject to the insults of a husband, to see the sacred work of the hands of maternal love degraded and denigrated, to see the pearl you cared for with such affection dirtied and dragged through the mud—oh!—that double blow is very heavy for a mother's heart and her dignity. I thought that my heart, having reached the highest point of pain, could not produce a new sorrow. But the heart is like a moist sponge that seems to have given out its last drop, but dispenses new ones if wrung once more. To live with sorrow has now become my natural state of affairs.

———◦◦◦———

Mme Sira to Mayda

See what society is with its prejudice, injustice, and merciless-ness. An anonymous letter and the shadow of a man in flight give a husband the right to condemn, to threaten, to think himself insulted, and to tear apart a heart and extinguish a life in order to preserve his honor. This is called the conduct of an honorable man.

People are dedicated to having their names respected. Fine. And every honorable person should have this right. But that name to which men give such importance, for which they make such a fuss, that name which they give to a woman, commanding her to watch unceasingly over its purity, I ask, in what condition does a man give that name—spotless or stained? And if it isn't spotless, then how would it be possible to keep clean something that has already been dirtied? Perhaps a woman would have the skill nec-essary to wipe out all blemishes—but in that case why should the stained act as judge over the unsullied? I suppose that the woman is a weak being because she must use a common name which is as degrading to the namer as to the named. So from this assumption that woman is weak, why is she subjected to such judgment if she herself is unable to resist, to compete, and to win? To perceive a weakness, to declare it, and then to display not even the slightest forgiveness regarding it is to go beyond the limits of merciless-ness. To be convinced of that weakness and yet to base the honor of one's name on it is the peak of contradiction. How could the preservation of a precious treasure be given over to weak hands? And if it is given over in this manner knowingly, who is to blame? So, in such circumstances, the claim of weakness should be taken into consideration, and if there is weakness we should abolish this intense abusive behavior that weighs heavily on women like the fatal verdicts of a military tribunal.

It is said that women are weak. Fine. But who says that men are not weak? In what way must I judge him and in which circumstances? A man walks about in immorality and degrades himself, but it matters not, for he is a man. So, a man is strong not when he appears virtuous, but when he corrupts his manliness. Breaking the vow of fidelity in marriage is as immoral for men as it is for women. In the smallest circumstances of life, breaking a promise is considered dishonorable. And so the responsibility for the mutually accepted agreement regarding the fidelity of two people sharing their lot belongs as much to the woman as to her husband. Have women granted permission for themselves to be deceived during the course of marriage? Not one of them has granted such permission, and yet men do not care a bit if they appear unfaithful. If someone has moral authority over those whom they call weak, are we to see the mark of that authority in the breaking of their promise?

People always argue that the immoral conduct of a woman has devastating consequences for the family. I ask: does a woman's guilt result from its consequences or, if not, then from her harming public morals by being unfaithful? But men are as responsible as women for the upkeep of public morals. Except for a class of women who bear only the name of their sex, women have within themselves the feeling of dignity of the highest order, through which they are strengthened. They have the taste of the beautiful and the sublime, through which they are elevated. Women carry out their duties as slaves, raising their dignity to that apex where men very often raise their names alone.

Women have always been imperfectly perceived. They have never been judged based on the truth, but rather in accordance with the times, spirit, social conditions, education and its consequences, passions, or mistakes. The Spartan woman does not resemble the Eastern one, as the Armenian woman[3] is not a European, as the primitive woman is neither Eastern nor European.

The courageous and pious women of Armenia would bless the God who deprives them of an easy life and subjects them to all sorts of catastrophes. They would die for the love of their God instead of enjoying a sweet life as apostates. The patriotic Spartan mother who would say to her child, "Be victorious or die," would of course not use such language in the well-adorned women's quarters where pleasures are showered down and fragrances are spread. Captive Jerusalem brought forth a Judith. The Rome of Lucretias and Brutuses brought forth a Cornelia. And from the French Revolution emerged Madame Roland and Charlotte Corday.

Isn't the child of a primitive woman born of a mother? And yet she sells the child with dry eyes, she is freed from the child as from a wearisome burden.

From these few examples it is easy to conclude that the woman presents contradictory images in various forms. Coming to the present time, we notice the frivolous woman occupied only with pleasure, the immoral woman occupied with gain, the hard-working woman with her fondness for appearances, the tradeswoman with goods, the virtuous woman citizen with the family, the studious woman with books, and the high-ranking noble woman with titles. When there is such a variety in the moral and social conditions of women, which of these is the generally accepted norm? Has it been decided in what form or color women should appear? How should a woman be seen—as a homemaker or as a student, a slave or freewoman, a public woman or citizen or mother? Has it been revealed how a woman should be? No. The upbringing received by a woman corresponds to which intention? What does it tend toward? Her upbringing disturbs her mind and causes her heart to err without giving any firm or direct principle or ideas that she can use to manage herself. She is led by prejudice, and she becomes a martyr. Not comprehending what great power, capacity, and actions can be produced by developing a woman's reason and moving her emotions, people condemn her. Nature has endowed woman with beautiful and favorable attributes, but violence and the law have disrupted these. Physical force—that is, brute advantage—has enslaved woman, and the law has strengthened her chains.

What does the law do, really? The law ties a rope around woman's neck that it tightens or loosens as need be. What is woman before the laws of the most civilized nation in Europe if not the property of her husband? She has no right to take any initiative, no will, no power, nor even permission to protest when her heart bleeds, or when her mind rebels. All protests against her stolen rights are a crime. Her lot is silence. In terms of pleasures, her husband has absolute advantage over her; in terms of punishment, he has parity with the law while there are excesses for women when it comes to being punished. The law pardons men for their vices, whereas the slightest transgression of a woman is strictly punished. Laws change with various contexts, they allow or restrain as need be. But the moral principles regarding women have always remained the same—the sovereign man, the slave woman.

Those grand principles that are declared in the European world, the principles of freedom and equality, are simply big words. What kind of equality is it that places half of humanity at the feet of men? What kind of freedom deprives women the right of protest, action, and the capacity to engage? What force tells men, "Act without fear, you are free," and tells women, "Caress your chains in silence"? Isn't it violence that allows the appropriation and enjoyment of what is not theirs? What does it matter if it is theft? What do the tears and sufferings of others matter? Or the rage that roars—without, however, being able to raise its voice—for they will force that daring mouth to silence, saying, "Lower your voice, for you are a woman, and it is not for you to enjoy what is our private domain. Take care of your children, serve our pleasures." It is in these conditions, beneath this degrading moral oppression—an oppression which transforms women—that people judge women's reason, feelings, capacities, circumstances, and passions, and proclaim a disastrous verdict against them. Wretched humanity.

When equality reigns between the two sexes in pleasure and punishment, in work and pay, then will the chains break apart, falsehood will cease, and society will gain in balance what it loses in the inequality of brute force. And from that balance, harmony is produced; from harmony, progress; and from progress, true enlightenment, which is the sum of intellectual and moral strength.

The Count to Mayda

Mayda, do you want to renounce this world and your loved ones by being buried in a convent? Do you want to be sacrificed? Fine. But have the bravery to sacrifice with you also the brother who worships you. Through you, the universe is mine. Without you, nothingness remains for me. You are the ear through which I hear, you are the mouth through which I speak. I have a heart that beats through you alone. Mayda, return the sparkle to my eyes, return the words to my mouth. Keep only my heart for yourself, for that is yours.

But if you are determined to carry out your sacrifice, let me know so that I may carry out mine at the same time. Don't worry that my complaint will disturb your monastic peace. I have always dreamed of your happiness. I would gladly suffer torture to see you happy. However, I cannot calmly watch that cold shroud that you are preparing to cover your warm heart. No, that I cannot accept. Only tell me, is it necessary to live or to die in this world? In death, as in life, you will always remain dear to me.

Mayda to Mme Sira

The truth has come out. Dikran is not at fault. They have deceived him in a cowardly manner. Dikran was not pretending—rather, he truly loved me. But, alas, for me he no longer exists. Terror and joy, darkness and light, life and death have taken over my whole being. What a moment that was when I discovered the truth! I rejoiced, only to feel my loss even more.

After those intense events that hurt her so much, my Houlianée gathered strength day by day and enjoyed happiness once more. It is true that Levon doted on her as in the past. However, I observed that a shadow of suspicion occasionally passed over his face, and he silently grieved.

One day when he was again sitting by my Houlianée and looking at her with loving eyes, he suddenly left with a perturbed expression. My daughter perceived nothing, but I quickly understood what had happened and went after him. He was taking a walk in the garden. I approached him to speak, when the sound of a revolver and, at almost the same time, a plaintive cry reached our ears from the grove's direction. Levon ran there and I went after him, where we shuddered to find a man drenched in blood, lying on the ground, and another person who was hurriedly running away. Herika was kneeling by the wounded man, who was Bedros T—, poor Hranush's father.

When we approached them, Herika rose and looked at me with hatred. And it seemed that the wounded man felt a fierce joy at seeing us, and, with vengeful eyes and a frothy mouth, he exclaimed, "Seize this woman!" pointing to Herika, "for she is the devil herself." Continuing, he said to me, "You, Madame, lost your Dikran because of her treachery, and you, sir, were to lose your Houlianée. I worshipped this woman, I was in a delirium, and there was no crime I wouldn't commit to win her heart, and I did everything to please her."

He fell silent, for the blood flowing from his massive wound weakened him. We took care of his wound, so that he was a bit relieved. Then he went on, "Let me finish my confession, for perhaps I will be unable to do so later. This woman loved Dikran and she could not bear that you, Madame, had conquered him. She promised her heart in return for her revenge, by which I was to separate Dikran from you. You lost a heart; I won a woman.

"I went and found Dikran, I disgraced your honor, and as proof of my lies, I showed him your ring that this wicked woman had stolen from my daughter's finger, cold with death. Dikran loved you, Madame, and despair drove him mad. However, your suffering as a lover was not enough for this wicked one. She wanted to strike at your maternal heart as well, and I served her evil purposes—for it was impossible for me not to carry out her will. I wrote that anonymous letter to your daughter, I was the one running away from the grove, and, if you want any more proof, here is Herika's letter," he said, extending it out to Levon.

"This place was our love nest. I came here before the appointed time, for this woman had bewitched me in such a manner that I wanted to breathe the air she breathes and to observe the house in which she lives. But imagine what indignation came over me when, in coming here, I found her in the arms of your neighbor Amaduni, the Armenian General, who is better known for his conquests in the world of love than on the battlefield. I looked at them without being seen, not wanting to believe my eyes at first—surprise and pain were blinding me so. But then I attacked this woman, wanting to kill her and her lover, when he emptied a revolver on me, threw me to the ground, and fled, leaving me with this woman who was repeating to me with filthy lips those insidious words that had once enchanted me. And now my hatred is as great as was my passion."

He ran out of breath, fell silent, and then continued, "Perhaps I will die in a few moments. You are right to hate me, both of you. I will take your curses with me, but I leave instead my revenge, which is also yours. Life is unbearable for me from now on. However, I wish to live in order to have the satisfaction of witnessing this monstrous woman's punishment."

He was unable to say more, for he was exhausted. On Levon's orders, he was picked up and taken to his home. It seemed that the wound was fatal. Although this man had been catastrophic for me, he was at the same time so miserable that it was impossible not to pity him. Is it even possible to hate someone who has fallen into the ditch of misfortune?

And what was I to say to Herika who, only a few hours before, was passing ostentatiously in front of me and now stood as a transgressor, though humbled, maintaining her haughtiness once more? She did not ask for a pardon, nor did she even utter a word to justify herself. She took on no remorseful manners, rather she listened to her condemnations with an untroubled face—as if the past events had nothing to do with her, standing speechless and motionless. Levon ordered her to follow him. She obeyed without displaying any shame, as if she were still mistress of the house. And the Armenian General Amaduni was rendered to justice by accepting his punishment for the crime.

When my daughter learned the details of this drama, she fell into my arms and said, "Poor mother! If you loved as I loved my Levon, how your noble heart must be broken." She asked Levon to immediately convey the affair to Dikran, "so that there would not be even a spot of dishonor upon my immaculate mother."

"O my Houlianée," Levon said, "that light which dispels my final doubt at the same time brings shame to our home. Herika can no longer be the wife of my brother nor can she even live beneath this roof."

When the insulted husband found out about his wife's reprehensible conduct, it was as if he had been struck by lightning, and he resembled a man whose life had unexpectedly been stolen from him. He worshipped Herika, but even so he said that he no longer wanted to have anything to do with dishonor. It was consequently decided to imprison her in a hospital. She left the house, always maintaining an unruffled expression, though she was as pale as death. It was impossible not to sympathize—seeing a woman endowed with the graces of nature, surrounded by all the advantages of society and perfectly master of herself, to be condemned to lose everything— alone, speechless and, head lowered, to waste away in scorn. What a downfall!

Since the very day that Herika left the house, it was as if her husband experienced a loss of sensation. He does not speak, nor does he allude to his misfortune. But beneath that calm exterior, it is clear that pain consumes him, for he has already been transformed.

I observe his sorrow and I am consoled, thinking that at least I was betrayed not by my Dikran but through fortune. I am relieved by this sad consolation. I imagine his despair when he eventually finds out about my innocence. Wasn't I right to think that Dikran could never be unfaithful? But what's the use? He lives, although dead to me. Perhaps the sighs of his heart respond to mine, and yet their echoes never meet, for the *impossible* stands as an expanse between them. Oh, I am not meant to be happy!

Verdant hope bestows only dry leaves in my hands, whereas it smiles upon others, abundantly distributing its gifts to them.

Mayda to the Count

Your selfless friendship, and the life that I owe you, have compelled me to express my gratitude to you. Therefore I sacrifice my peace to you, and I will remain in the world of the living so as not to condemn you to the monastic life I had in mind. Instead of dying in consolatory silence, let me die for all to see, hearing the unbearable noises of this world. You also came to know the soul's wounds, Count, as did I. Do not get upset with me if I am unable to cure them. Who wants to have sighs and tears as their lot, renouncing the good of the world? My heart was taken over by such love that it exhausted all of its essence in feeling. Nothing remains now, and although I am young I still bow my head upon the grave as a wispy willow. How easy it would be for me if you lived in my country and if I could relieve my pain with yours! The burden of life seems lighter when it leans upon two people. O Count, I sacrificed my final consolation for you. If only my renunciation of peace could provide you with some peace. I feel no regret about my sacrifice because I was able to save a victim like you.

Mme Sira to Mayda

So you became the unfortunate plaything of a deceitful woman, is that it? A wicked shadow opened a precipice between two loyal hearts that forgetting alone can close, and yet can it be filled so soon? Time—that miraculous healer which can cure all ailments—will treat yours as well, but who could ever fully wipe out the black stamp of misfortune?

Herika was driven away from the conjugal home as punishment for her misdeeds. I would have found that treatment enough if it were not for the evil machinations and their catastrophic consequences. But when they imprison a woman in a hospital as punishment for her infidelity to her husband, it is difficult for me to justify that treatment, because that same infidelity has become the daily transgression of men and has turned into such a natural thing that it does not even receive any mention.

Now, I ask, with what right do they deprive Herika of her personal freedom? With what right do they condemn her to pass her days in a prison that perhaps will be her grave in the end? With what right do men act as the executioners of women for a transgression that they continuously carry out in the open almost without punishment? Who gave them permission to act freely and the absolute ability to oppress women for that same freedom—who gave them that right? Nature? No, because it bestowed the same qualities, the same passions, the same virtues, and the same vices to both sexes. Why, then, what man believes to be just for himself is considered shameful when it comes to the opposite sex, and whatever seems objectionable and contemptible about women is not as deserving of scorn when applied to him? Anything that violates the sanctity of family is a crime. Anything that disturbs public morals is an insult to humanity. Anything that is a vice for women is a vice for men as well, and the consequence, though different, is nonetheless just as miserable—harmful both for the peace of the family and for social morals. So men want to use their vices as a special power to oppress the opposite sex. This absolute power affirms two issues. First, it clearly demonstrates the extent of women's disgraced position, which causes them to remain indifferent to their infringed dignity. Second, it reveals the unforgivable selfishness of men that reasonable thought and justice condemn.

———⊃ ⋅ ◆ ⋅ ⊂———

Dikran to Mayda

O Mayda, I got to know you at first to worship you, to believe you to be mine, and then to lose you, to pine away with sighs, to curse you out loud, and to worship you in secret. I have been the victim of a devastating conspiracy. I thought the angel of purity to be impure, virtue to be vice, beauty to be ugliness, faithfulness to be treachery. My heart was roaring with impossible fury, it was bleeding, it was rebelling against you and your image, and it sought another heart as support, as a hand to look after the wound that was constantly open. They tore my heart apart and I afflicted yours. I tried to devote my love to another, but it resisted, it remained for you and it will always beat for you alone.

Tell me, Mayda, what is left for me to do in such a desperate situation as mine? The beautiful and pure Mayda is alive and free, whereas I am not at liberty. My chains have never appeared as heavy as now. I would move all the earth in order to have you, and yet I am unable to break apart the chains that I myself forged and that I hate with my whole being. I am speaking only of my bitter condition without recalling the sorrow that I caused you, the tears that you shed. You came to Paris to find me. But I, believing you to be false, was in too much of a hurry to replace your image with that of another in order to punish it. My mouth cursed you, but my heart always worshipped you. The cause of our catastrophe—Herika—is paying for her crimes at present. But what's the use? Does her punishment return my Mayda to me? I know you suffered a lot, my poor angel, in considering me unfaithful. Did you curse me as I did you? To love you and make you weep, to worship you and send you away, to place a dreadful expanse between the two of us—this was the work I carried out.

Take pity, have mercy on the miserable one who does not know whether to be hurt or overjoyed at your innocence, and who finds a treasure only to lose it once again. Have mercy on the unfortunate one who, with his own hands, brought about our own misery. Take pity! Mayda, forgive me, love me once again if you had stopped loving me, for your love will be the beacon of my dark night. Take pity! They fooled me in a cowardly manner, judge for yourself.

They accused you of unfaithfulness. I wrote you to ask for information, and my letter went unanswered. Then I traveled, and when I returned to Paris, thinking I might finally receive news from you, how great was my pain when my expectations were frustrated! I dispatched a second letter to you as well and was met with the same silence, whereupon I definitely concluded that you had forgotten me. Who in my condition would not have been the victim of such a wicked deception? I was a lost man for more than six months. Fallen into the ocean of despair, I had become the plaything of its roaring waves. I sought a harbor for salvation. I asked for a merciful hand to save me and, when I found that hand, instead of salvation, I found chains; instead of life, death. Mayda, how miserable I am! Take pity!

When I came across you at the church and saw you faint, I was so strongly moved that my companion observed my anxiety with dread and grew suspicious. I forgot that I had an unfortunate witness next to me, I forgot your treachery to me, I ran toward you. I wept kneeling by you, I worshipped you while cursing you, I took care of you with compassion. And as you were about to regain consciousness, I left you, unwillingly leaving my heart to you. Oh, I madly loved you despite believing you to be false. Take pity, Mayda, take pity!

—⟶◆⟵—

Mayda to Dikran

You ask for my pity when you hurt my heart deeply and bathed it in its blood; when, sprinkling the drops of blood flowing from my wound, you boldly played with them. You ask for pity when, after feasting your eyes on the terrible sight of my sorrows, you made a guillotine and placed my heart there, striking a devastating blow on it without destroying it, so that I may live and be tormented. You ask for pity, but did you pity me when I came, crossing the seas, in order to find you in a remote country and to discover the reason for your silence, when I was lying on the ground almost lifeless upon hearing that your impatient heart had found another love to take my place? Did you have mercy on me when I was between life and death for almost three weeks, abandoned to strange hands? Did you have mercy on me when, worshipping an unfaithful one like you, I had decided to bury myself in a convent and to cry over you who were dead to me? Did you have mercy on me when, calling out your name, I was constantly shedding my tears to the night, my only friend and confidant? Tell me, did you offer me the pity that you request? You denied our love, per-secuted my memory, and without any qualms you passed on to someone else the loving promises you had made to me.

Didn't you feel any doubt in being unfaithful? You deceived the heavens, you deceived the earth, you deceived your heart and my heart, and you call for pity! You presented an adversary to my terrified eyes, while I—left alone, abandoned—remained faithful to you. I declined being the companion in fortune to the person who hosted me in my suffering, who took care of me during my illness, and who offered me a heart, titles, and wealth. I declined everything, for I was unable to take back what I had already devoted to you. It was rightfully yours and, against your will, I kept my love for you. Compare your conduct with mine and tell me, were you as miserable as I? Did you love me as I loved you? And do you have the right now to appeal to my pity? I never cursed you, but instead always blessed you. So then keep happiness for yourself, leave the tears to me.

We have an obligation to fulfill on this earth, to make happy the person who has become a companion in fortune. She is innocent, and she has the right to demand your affection. Love her. It would never please me to have my memory disturb her peace. Instead of one miserable being, don't bring about two, and don't teach her to curse my name as you taught yourself.

When one day my sorrow-stricken heart finally finds some rest in the bosom of death, I wish that she too will mix her tears with yours. If she robbed me of that being whom I loved so much, was she to blame? And do I have the right to condemn her for a matter in which she has no fault at all? Farewell, Dikran. I loved you alone and I will never love another. Your image will go to the grave with me. Think of me as already dead and buried, and remember without any pangs of guilt our past beautiful days which slid by so quickly. But no, I do not want to die without granting you forgiveness. It seems to me that my sleep on my deathbed will be restless. So I forgive you from the heart. Farewell once again, Dikran.

⸺◦◦◦⸺

Mayda to Mme Sira

The Count arrived. Being near a loyal friend is a source of happiness for me. And the Count, it seems, is being reborn with every moment and enjoying the beauties of the Bosphorus to the

116

full. The Bosphorus is enchanting, he says, with all its various sights—here with a beautiful and pleasant coastline that looks like a gulf, and a little further a lake. The heights with colorful houses and mosques especially surprise him, as do the slim minarets which seem, he says, held up in the air by an invisible hand. He finds the European shore to be wonderful but he especially appreciates the verdant hillocks of Asia, which seem to be competing with the wonders on the opposite shore for beauty, color, and light, finally emerging victorious. Likewise with the white pavilions scattered about the mountains, which appear to be giant bouquets of flowers. The splendid palaces of Oriental style, the fortresses in ruins which seem to be the gray-haired guardian spirits of the Bosphorus, the constant movement of boats large and small, which have an effect on the sea as if they were wandering islands—all of this the Count observes with wonderstruck eyes. But what captures his soul in particular are the Muezzins. It is as if they declare the greatness of God out of the air. Never has a prayer, he says, reached such heights as the Muslim sound of the glorification which is released on high as a bouquet of harmony, fading into infinity. Christianity does not have anything as noble and heartfelt as this call from the soul, which takes the place of arid bell-ringing.

One night, the moon was shining high above. Myriads of stars were surrounding it, as if the sea was tumbling gilded pieces, so bright and resplendent was the moon. Nothing disturbed the surface of the water, rather everything was peaceful and mystical. Suddenly the voice of the Muezzin slid as a shudder through space. Without speaking, we lent it our ears with boundless enchantment, when the Count, his heart moved, broke the silence, saying, "Mayda, I wish to have this prayer as an accompaniment to death, and the ocean as a grave." He exclaimed, "Let us die because we cannot find happiness on this earth." It was as if an invisible force was pushing him in that direction.

I was standing troubled and speechless, without being able to calm my heart's emotions. "What foolishness!" he said, immediately coming to his senses, "Is it not merciless to wish to bury so much heavenly grace beneath a relentless shroud?" My daughter approached us at that time with cheerful cries, as if putting an end to a morbid thought.

Our days calmly passed by in intimate conversation or enchantment with the miracles of nature. Being weak, I find it impossible to walk around for long. Because the Count would not be content with taking a walk alone, I felt obliged to accompany him. I suggested that we visit the nearby Hagia Sophia Church, that wonderful temple of Christianity.

The majesty of the Church built by Constantine in Byzantine style, the grandeur of its execution, the walls of jasper and porphyry, the hundred columns brought over from the temple at Ephesus, the eight domes upon the tallest of which an immense cross is noticeable until now, the spoiled faces of four angels with their wings spread, and finally the total perfection of the splendid edifice astonished the Count. We found especially curious the name of the Doge of Venice, Enrico Dandolo, on a Latin engraving on the marble floor in one corner on the right of the vast women's gallery. This Doge had come to Constantinople in the 13th century at the request of Alexius Angelus, whose father, Isaac Angelus, had been deposed by his brother and forcibly imprisoned. After pushing out the dictator, the Crusaders and Enrico Dandolo settled in Constantinople, which marked the beginning of Latin rule. We could not understand how Dandolo's name came to be on that stone.

When we passed the Hippodrome, I said, "This place, where a mild and industrious people calmly walks about today, was formerly meant for horse races, and scores of spectators would crowd here to express their support for some competing party or the other, rewarding the victor with ardent applause.

"The most important of those parties were the Greens and the Blues, who had become the main objects of public support, and who would crown or depose kings with full authority. While they were fighting—calling out, 'Nika!', that is, 'Win!'—the Greens and the Blues threw Justinian down from his throne, then placing Hypatius on it, who paid for his brief rule by dying in the waters of the Bosphorus. During this confusing time, the Hippodrome was set on fire, as was the Hagia Sophia, the dome of which was later reconstructed by an Armenian named Tiridates. Justinian ascended the same throne once again by the hands of the Blues, who had deposed him. Likewise those wonderful baths adorned through the care of Constantine the Great, as well as four thousand splendid homes, were devoured by the flames. Standing here is that celebrated column which is formed by three snakes twisted around one another, the heads completely cut off. They say that after the sea battle at Salamis, Themistocles offered that column to Apollo and placed it at his renowned temple, which is in Delphi. They also affirm that Constantine moved this masterpiece to Constantinople."

I thought it necessary to have the Count visit the Janissaries[4] both because of the importance of the historical role they played and for the interesting appearance of their uniforms. "These people who do not speak were the dread and terror of the Sultans," I said. "It is as if they still threaten the rulers in their silence. A signal from the Janissaries was enough for thrones to fall, heads to roll, blood to flow, and unbridled revolutions to fail. When the Sultans formed military units for their security, they did not realize that one day they would tremble beneath the strong hands of this armed force. But Sultan Mahmud, instead of trembling beneath the swords continuously brandished above his head, destroyed the powerful Janissaries with a daring blow—their bloodied heads left floating on the Bosphorus, staining its waters red. And at that same moment, the royal seat of the Sultans was free." These brief details filled the Count with indescribable joy, for it was pleasant for him to hear once again from me events related to the history of the Turks.

We cast a glance at those beautiful gardens descending in steps to the shore of the mixed waters of the Bosphorus and the Marmara. "In these gardens," I said to the Count, "would soar Constantine's well-adorned palace, not a trace of which remains today. That royal dwelling bore witness over time to the acts of bravery, the debaucheries, the indolence, and the religious debates of the rulers. The rulers would incite these debates for the sake of their personal interests, inflaming people with discord. That palace bore witness to the gradual deterioration and destruction of the Byzantine Empire. It bore witness to the moment when the last Constantine took arms in defense of the homeland, mixing his final breath with that of the Byzantine Empire."

I continued: "Nothing remains now of Constantine's rich mansion except a memory, and only these four walls from the summer residence of the Palaeologues[5]—silent witnesses to glorious days past." Although I was tired, I wanted to show the Count one of our Armenian institutions, that is, the standing memory of the past strength and patriotism of Harutiun Bezjian—I was referring to our Hospital, where hundreds of the ill and unfortunate find remedy and shelter, as the deserted child finds protection and education. The usefulness of an institution is not to be judged by its opulence and decorations, but rather by the services it renders. Our Armenian hospital is one of those. I took pride in it as foreigners do in their wonderful constructions. The Count not only comprehended the legitimacy of my patriotic feelings, but he especially applauded them.

However I concealed from the Count the blameworthy indifference of our Nation regarding such a holy place, where the gray-haired finds protection, the ill finds healing, and the orphan finds mercy. I did not tell him we owe to particular virtuous and patriotic individuals alone the occasional praiseworthy arrangements as well as the humanitarian care. I did not say that this place, to which every Armenian heart was to fervently offer a small portion—I did not tell him, I say—that this place had many times been the center of pillage and injustice, that the bread, clothing, and small portion offered to the poor had benefited the pleasures of some particular persons. I did not tell him that the bitter smile of the needy, the sigh of the unfortunate, and the tears of the orphan had met there the mercilessness of corrupt individuals instead of finding a brother's heart. I kept quiet about all these things, for the Armenian dregs gush forth upon us in some way as well—we too become sullied because we are a part of the whole.

Finally passing through impossibly winding roads and subject to the constant tremors of the carriage, we arrived at the shore, where, boarding a boat, we dashed over the waters, still holding on to the effects of the various influences we bore.

When we reached the royal Dolmabahçe Palace, I said to the Count, "Here is a place that contains the entire story of the human heart." I added: "In order to appear sympathetic to a royal master, how many men kept vigil, worked, made enemies, defeated enemies, were overthrown by enemies even when they seemed to have reached the pinnacle of their dreams! In order to please their crown-adorned master, how many women expended their efforts, were loved, were left alone deserted, cried, and suffered over the advantage of their rivals when they thought themselves to be powerful mistresses of the royal heart! So many were tortured by a word, by a glance directed at some other beauty who eventually would succeed her in the master's heart! Yes, so many have wept. But who counted those tears of the heart? Who gave them any importance? Perhaps they may be considered drops of water, but they were drops filled with the bitterness of the heart. When those unlucky beauties were yet full of vigor, they would feel the emaciation, withering, and weakening of their hearts. And then one day they stopped beating. Death killed what was grace, what was freshness, what was life. Who observed that murder? It was just the loss of some being who had been succeeded by some other beauty. Yes, it was just the loss of some being, but it was a heart that had cried, sighed, and bled. Who gathered that final breath wherein the entire history of that sad story was contained? A grave is dug to receive a young woman whom hope had graced and despair had killed. Passers-by discovering that a woman of youth rests there, say, 'A pity. It was yet too soon to die,' and continue their way. Can people be thought to have died too soon when they know misery and, when already thought to be old in their youth, is not death indeed a consolation for them? Answer me, Count," I asked, "do you not also feel old like me?"

"Mayda," he said, "life is a big teardrop that a sunbeam warms in order to quickly evaporate it. Each person has a cup of bitterness which the present empties and the future fills. The cups of some overflow—this is the only difference. You suffered a great deal, and think yourself the unluckiest one. You are mistaken, for people count only their own tears. Is my misfortune not indeed as heavy as yours? You lose a treasure and the same happens with me. For you as with me, there is an additional someone in between. To suffer means to feel; to feel is to live. Suffering marks strongly each moment of life, for we are born to live."

"Life," the Count continued, "is a vast precipice in which the terrified eye sees the night. My soul is obliged to descend to its bottom, for a ruthless hand forcibly pushes it there. Love illuminates that precipice with its rays of light only to make the darkness thicker later when it extinguishes the torch it holds with its frigid breath."

The Count fell silent, and I listened until he stopped speaking. Suddenly, as he dipped his hand in the sea and raised it, a few drops hung from his fingers and then fell into the sea and were lost. "Here is the image of people," he said, "they are tied to life for a moment, and then they are tossed about to become lost in the general whole from which they sprang."

Our boat was gliding on the water, and at times we observed with wonder the dynamic infinity that gently lulled us in its bosom, and at other times, the blue infinity that was spread above our heads. And we—as atoms between these two spaces— we would rise in our thoughts with one and would bow down with the other. We arrived at our dwelling as the moon crossed the horizon to bewitch nature, and the sound of the Muezzin enthusiastically welcomed it.

Dikran to Mayda

So then you forgive me, my charming Mayda. My heart is relieved, but it cannot find its lost happiness. Everything is unbearable for me, especially that innocent being whose only transgression is loving me very much, for any love—except for yours—is hell to me. I truly sympathize with that poor one who has become my companion in fortune, but I loathe that mouth which calls me "my Dikran." And yet everything gives her the right to call me that. My soul alone protests and will always protest. My emotions in the church betrayed me too much, and I try in vain to hide my indifference toward her which overtakes me. When I see her tears, I truly pity her. But my fingers wipe those tears away while my soul curses them—I would move and throw off everything in order to have you, and yet merciless fortune, or a woman, or some devil overcame and destroyed me.

Mayda, as a final favor, listen to my supplications and let Dikran enjoy your voice one last time, let him see your graces one last time, let him think you his for a moment and, if necessary, let him die at your feet. Bestow your forgiveness, allow me to recount my pain, and then you will judge for yourself if I am worthy of your sympathy as I am of the pity I requested from you, for you are an angel and angels always know how to forgive.

Mayda, I beg favors for an unfortunate being. Permit me to appear as guilty before you. Has the Dikran you worshiped become so hateful to you as to altogether expel him from your sight? Say that you will allow me to see you, and I will immediately come. I will fly, I will enjoy life for a moment in order to bear death every day thereafter.

Mme Sira to Mayda

I am glad that the Count's arrival put an end, temporarily, to your solitary life. Your thoughts on the greatness and glories of nations, as well as the causes of their downfall, adequately affirm my belief that a nation's progress is carried out through work, with all of its attributes, whereas its destruction is a consequence of indolence and vice. Anything that belongs to nations belongs also to every individual, because the strength of society is formed by the sum of individual powers. Now I ask you, Mayda, what do you get from your inactivity and who gains from your life? What is the service you are rendering to your nation, to humanity, that wipes out all the distinctions between peoples? What is the sorrow you are relieving? Where are your thoughts focused? Each intellectual flicker of yours, each beat of your heart, is meant to join the entirety of human radiance and feelings.

I gave you time to soothe your pain. But if you want to continue to live in the same condition, in the end you will be unable to be revived, because evil will take root and it is difficult to uproot what is firmly in place. The more you submit to the violence of sorrow, the more violently it acts upon you. Face it, rush on it, and you will turn out to be the victor. But tell me, who promised you happiness on this earth? Who has ever been perfectly happy so that you too may be so? The smallest to the largest have known suffering. Geniuses, who are the benefactors of humanity, have been subjected to ingratitude, prison, exile, and death. These immortal martyrs of knowledge and work would give us light and life, and in return they would accept death. We are the wrestlers of life. Whether diligent or not, we are wounded, only to stand on our feet once again and to compete, using the strength that remains in us.

We have no right to say, "This is where my work ends. Here, in my arena, I stand; I no longer want to move forward." No, you do not have that right, for that behavior is moral suicide, and yet you loathe suicide because you think that you yourself do not have the power to end the life bestowed on you. But you don't have any pangs of conscience about weakening your moral, vital essence little by little through inaction, abandoned to an imperceptible suicide. The courage of any suicide—physical or moral—is a reprehensible courage, because living and competing is much more honorable than putting an end to a tempestuous life in a moment of despair, or gradually destroying its vital essence.

Life is a battlefield, and people are the ones who wage war. Does the wounded soldier have the right to flee from the battle when his wound has healed somewhat and he is able to brandish a weapon once again? If he flees, he is an unforgivable deserter. Are the deserters of life any less reprehensible? Don't you feel that people aspire to rise above the events that crush them and say, "I scorned them, I stand upright, and instead of being beaten, I have emerged the victor—for I am useful, for I act, for I am a human being"?

You would of course also apply these thoughts of mine to someone suffering like you. But you have become the living dead, so much so that you don't have the ability to feel the condition that is causing you disgrace. Through the inactivity of your intellectual and moral state, you are changing your appearance day by day, you are succumbing, you are gradually descending the steps of morality, and a day will come when, as you approach the condition of an animal, you will appear as the personification of an animal-human. What purpose does your reputation serve you, Mayda, when you succumb as the weakest creature?

Mayda to Mme Sira

Blame me with the same injustice for both my unwilling silence and my extreme inactivity. Pay attention to what I have to say and then tell me if I appear guilty to you.

The Count left after being my guest for three months. He will make the necessary arrangements to come to settle in Constantinople and look over me as a selfless brother. These are truly beautiful thoughts and worthy of his noble heart. But it remains to be seen whether those resolutions can be carried out, for although my efforts and courage to withstand the affliction consuming my life are great, I feel myself weaken day by day by an implacable illness. The Count already noticed my condition and exhorted me to pass the winter in a temperate climate, promising to accompany me everywhere. He also offered me a share in his wealth, insisting that a brother has the right to make such a gift for a sister (especially one who could sacrifice her monastic peace). I absolutely declined such a proposal, and his insistence did not change my decision at all. He would become upset at this rejection of mine, as would I at his oft-repeated pleas. It is true that this was a new demonstration of his inexhaustible nobility.

When the Count departed, I was deeply moved, and my weakness intensified as well. You understand, of course, that it was impossible to look with indifferent eyes at the emptiness that an unparalleled friend had filled for three months. I was pondering by myself when I saw Levon approaching with an expression of uncontrollable emotion.

"What's going on, Levon? You look intensely angered," I said.

"I'm afraid," he replied, "that we will be subject to new catastrophes, for Herika has found a way to escape from prison. Her guard insists on not being an accomplice to that escape and nothing more, and efforts at finding that woman have remained fruitless so far. That noxious woman, who felt no pangs of conscience in committing injustices—what won't she do now that she has a score to settle? You know already that Bedros T— paid for her love with his life. Then what will we pay for that woman's hatred?"

These words filled me with terror. If I were certain that I would be the martyr of Herika's vengeance, I would remain completely unconcerned. But until now she did not wish for my death, rather she wanted to hurt me by aiming her arrows at my loved ones. Can I live without fear for my Houlianée? Can I count on Dikran being in safety? My sleep is troubled with terrifying dreams, and my days with anxiety. It is as if I can see the new catastrophes that Herika's indignation prepares for us in the dark. I think about meeting her menacing and blazing eyes. I think that each moment will give birth to fatal forms, and every passing moment cannot secure me against the one that follows. An unfortunate event kills someone in one blow, but anxiety kills slowly, making one feel the bitterness of each blow.

Now, my dear, tell me—are courage and wishful thinking enough to overcome my rightful fears and despair? How would you want me to think, or to act, when my mind runs constantly from my Houlianée to Dikran, when each sound, each movement, terrifies me, and I look restlessly into everyone's face with the fear of hearing bad news? O my God, so much suffering for just a few days of life!

⎯⎯⌂·◆·⌂⎯⎯

Mayda to Dikran

It is impossible for you to see me, Dikran. Keep the gift you want to bestow upon me for someone else, who has legitimate rights over you. What do your mistakes matter to her? You affirm your indifference to your poor spouse, but, in seeing me, do you hope to relieve that? We make the present worse by reviving the thought of our lost bliss. Do I have the right to win a heart that is no longer mine? And won't I be subject to rightful reproach in my wanting to win that heart and also in adding to your spouse's already sizeable misfortune? Who could know you without loving you, and what kind of a dreadful condition is it to love without being loved?

No, Dikran, we must not see each other again. Our mutual condition itself demands this sacrifice. Separating after seeing each other will be all the more unbearable. To hear your voice, to see your form, to gather this world in me for a moment, and then to lose everything—no, no, I am unable to endure such a trial. O unlucky Mayda! What right do you have to consider as yours the sanctified belonging of another? I don't have that right even for a moment, although I would sacrifice my life for it. No, Dikran, you will see me no more. Let us flee far from one another, although our hearts constantly yearn to be closer to each other. I do not want to abandon my conscience and duties, rather I want to die at the hour of death at least with a clear conscience, for that will be the only consolation I will take with me to the grave. You are unable to rob me of this consolation. And even if you could do so, I would flee from you. How could I have such a fierce ability to compete with my heart?

Farewell, Dikran!

Mme Sira to Mayda

So much emotion, so many storms rumble around you, exhausting you. Bear with your fiery imagination and do not torment your mind with sad images. With the influence of Levon's good social standing, you will of course soon succeed in seizing that wicked woman without giving her enough time to harm you.

How desirable it would be if you could get away from Constantinople for a while, if you could come here to Corfu and spend the winter, for the sake of your health and peace of mind. But I easily understand that your maternal heart cannot be away from her child when it considers her in danger. What a consolation it would have been to enjoy your presence in my solitude, to relieve you and be relieved by you! A dream!

In the meantime, I have made some new acquaintances. A Turk I know, thanks to whom a complicated affair of mine was settled some time ago, has temporarily settled here and become my neighbor because of a slight personal weakness. He has two beautiful wives, one of whom is a miracle of nature. I had never seen such a perfect height, such a stunning complexion, and such expressive eyes, mixed with grace in her movements, more reminiscent of a queen than a delicate woman. She also has quite a polished mind, through which her company has become pleasant for me.

This beautiful woman had a husband, of whose jealousy she has been the miserable victim. Unable to withstand the daily martyrdom, she fled from her married home with the help of a friend on the very day that her husband was going to a faraway country with work and was forcing her to go with him. Through her friend, she found a place to stay at the home of this Turkish acquaintance of mine, where she was ruling as a lady due to her singular beauty.

So this is the story of her life.

I discovered however that the older of these two rivals is pining away in envy, noticing that the newly arrived woman is in full control over her husband. And I will not be surprised at all if I find out one day that they have thrown that poor victim out of the house. Her beauty and graces appear dimmed under the influence of anxiety, whereas her adversary is adorned even more with her victory.

There is nothing that goes against social order as much as polygamy, which is nothing more than a heart which becomes an object of competition among numerous women. The happiness of a family home is formed by the intimate relationship between two souls, participating in that silent pact with each other's sorrows and joys, living for the very same life, interests, yearnings, and being reborn through their children. What trust can be held by a woman who constantly fears the power of a rival and who finds in her husband not a friend, but a master to whose whims she is obliged to resign herself? She is a mother, but someone else is as much of a mother under the same roof. Her heart, self-esteem, benefits, everything is subject to danger, and her life is a relentless storm. Love, submission, and selflessness are requested of that poor woman, but for what in return? Daily favors are her reward.

And what happens to the selfless heart that does not wait for the reward of love? Doesn't the heart have its own laws?

Who listens to its soft sighs and covert rebellions? Who sees its despairs and vendettas? Peace is assumed with silence. But the mountain that carries out volcanic activities inside—what does it emit when it stirs its fiery waves within? What can those feelings be, the ones that are wiped out, or inflamed, or have become bitter with the constant presence of the antagonist? If the woman loves in these conditions, her life is an everlasting martyrdom. And if she does not love, it is continuous disgust, daily artifice, a machine for piling wealth by pillaging one's master and thereby securing the future—meaning it is a base exchange. Polygamy is the pinnacle of women's debasement, a condition of martyrdom. It is the absence of love, it is family anarchy. Each rival mother wants to gather fatherly favors for her child. Consequently, hatred creeps into brothers born of various mothers, they become each other's enemies, and the father's house serves as a nest for opposition and evil, which more and more poison different intentions.

The new bride of my acquaintance is so certain of her power that it is as if she scorns any rival. But however great her influence, can she look untroubled to the future? Can she be assured that some other graceful being will not cause her the sorrows she has brought about?

I was lately speaking with my neighbor about the unlawful conditions produced by polygamy. Although he is quite a serious man, he had difficulty in understanding what I was saying. He thought that his first wife was very happy because she enjoyed all the pleasures of life, and that her peace was not disturbed at all by the advantages with which the other was being favored. "What does she lack?" he would say continuously. There are many men who think that the fortune of women is complete when they enjoy the material benefits of life. They do not understand, or they do not want to understand, that a woman has a heart, and that her happiness or unhappiness stems from it. How few are those who understand this truth.

We speak of you with that beautiful and graceful woman, and each time she expresses great pleasure. Imagine what joy it is for me to occupy myself with a matter that I love! Nothing is more comforting during times of absence than to speak of those people who are sacred to us. It is as if the bitterness of distance is partly mitigated, and we feel special sympathy to people with whom we can pass our time sharing the same pleasant subject. Perhaps I would not have found this enchanting woman so pleasant if she did not listen to my stories about you with such sympathetic attention. Perhaps there is some exaggeration in the interest she shows about you and the motivation for that conduct is her desire to be dear to me, for I have understood that she is very shrewd. I do not know whether it is the enjoyment of my company or her wish to remain far from her hated rival that causes her to frequent my house so much.

<hr />

Mayda to Mme Sira

In this doubtful state I could never bear a separation from my Houlianée. Imaginary monsters would appear more colossal at a distance, and it would continuously appear to me that my daughter had been martyred to treachery. I know that travel and especially your loving companionship would be very beneficial to me because my health is failing. How I have changed! If you knew, of course you would be pained, and were I to visit you that beautiful woman of yours would never worry that she would lose her charms to me. Consequently, she would perhaps share with me the sympathy that, I am sure, she has devoted to you already. But I honestly confess that I have a particular feeling toward that other being, persecuted by fortune, for I feel that all unlucky ones are sisters. I don't know with whom I am united through the ties of suffering. I notice my tears in theirs and I hear my sighs in their own.

The efforts expended at finding Herika have remained fruitless so far. It is as if her memory is the foreboding image of a hair-raising specter that constantly surrounds me night and day. When I am besieged by darkness, it seems that flames gush out of my adversary's mouth, they cast flares of a Dantean inferno upon me and, blade in hand, with a horrific smile, she threatens my loved ones. I am filled with dread, and my hair stands on end.

So many times in my sleep I thought that I saw my daughter struggling beneath Herika's oppression and her cry of despair. One night in particular I thought that I was seated by Dikran and silently looking at his face in wonder, when suddenly Herika attacked me and drove a sword into my breast. I asked Dikran for mercy, but I awoke terrified and he was no longer there.

This unmerciful sight intensifies in my heart day by day. I don't know why, but instead of being wiped out, it adds new sorrows to my past pain. We are two hearts wandering on the ocean of life, pushed far from each other by opposing winds. The days and nights follow each other in vain. Nothing brings us closer together. There is a precipice between the two of us—death alone can fill it. So death will wipe out the traces of an indelible image, death alone will be the conqueror of love when neither time nor distance managed to overcome it. Dikran! My sighs dissipate into eternity without giving an echo of love. In vain do I look around, in vain am I attentive—nothing, nothing! Despair stands before me as the skeleton of mercilessness and with perfidious rejoicing presents an image that it snatches away when I try to approach it.

Life, life! What a mysterious word! What a world of misery, tears, bitter pleasures, darkness, and dull light! What an intertwining of envy, deceit, and falsehood—these spread with irresistible flows like lava from mountains of fire. They burn, raze, and destroy everything besides truth and virtue, two terrible, tremendous, and celestial columns which stand and resist as support to the Eternal.

Creation appears to be based on the harmony of general love. Is there a better way of saying this? Thus the sun is light in its entirety, the flower is fragrance, and the brook is murmur. The sun causes the plant to bear fruit, the plant shelters the bird, and this winged musician enlivens the sacred silence of the forests with its warbling, and then, fluttering in the brook and drinking drops of its clear water, it quenches its thirst. So people alone are exceptions to this general law. They alone can conceive the sword, tear hearts to pieces, sharpen the iron, spill blood, and leave behind only traces of tears wherever they appear and pass through. So people alone are the spirit of evil, and yet they have hearts to love and souls to worship you, O my God.

Heavenly love—divine source through which everything is cleansed and from which virtue springs forth victorious! Love—source of tears! Love—that sparkle which is a gift of heaven—always illuminate my soul struck by darkness, be the beacon of my short-lived days! O Love! You abandoned my heart to perdition, yet you are ever sacred to me . . .

My dear, forgive me for pouring out my soul. Perhaps it is the final cry to love, to you, to God. I was feeling that my soul was oppressed beneath its burden. Oh! I wanted to relieve it by letting out a desperate cry.

Dikran to Mayda

The very same day took my wife and my child from me. The mother died after giving birth to the child. I was going to name my daughter Mayda. But I was a father for only two hours. The death of the child was followed by the death of the mother.

When the unlucky woman reached her final moments, she was holding my hand in hers, asking for forgiveness for unwillingly being the cause of my misfortune. After the event in the church, I felt like a brute because I had been unable to conceal the flame devouring me.

I understood the depth of the bitterness with which that selfless soul must have been filled—I felt a sincere regret. Through tender caring I had tried to make her forget the catastrophic past. Oh, Mayda! Am I born for the misfortune of others? That poor being asked to be together with her child in the same coffin and grave. "If I was a mother for only two hours," she said, "let me at least remain a mother in eternity." With a final loving acknowledgment, she took her last breath in my arms.

Cruelly tortured by my conscience, I stood motionless by the dead body of that heartbroken being, and with pain I noticed the remains of so much beauty and youth. Perhaps my indifference was the cause of her death. Perhaps I opened an incurable wound in her mother's heart. Did the unlucky mother know when she was giving her daughter away as a bride that she was handing her over to the bosom of death? Oh, Mayda, Mayda! How much shedding of tears have I caused in my life!

The mother rests with her little child in the shade of a willow, and the murmur of the wistful leaves lulls their eternal sleep.

Such a blow, such pangs of conscience would have been enough to poison my life—if your adored memory did not relieve me. So I am free and I reach you, stepping over two graves. So you are mine. No longer will you mercilessly deny me. No, it is not a dream. You are mine, Mayda! My heart has always been yours, and the blows of fate never had any effect on it. With my love I will wipe out the traces of the sorrows that I caused you. I don't know whether I am awake or the plaything of a dream?

I will see you soon once again. But the hours drift by so slowly, it is as if time has stood still forever. Each moment I spend away from you is a precious moment stolen from my happiness. Whoever has been oppressed by fortune as much as I have ultimately has the right to be worthy of its smile.

———◇———

Mme Sira to Mayda

How could such an enchanting body contain such a black soul? My beautiful neighbor, not wanting to tolerate even the presence of her defeated rival, had her thrown out of her married home. This poor victim of jealousy laments the loss of a selfless husband in silence and solitude. It is true that he looks after his wife's needs, but he never visits her and finds happiness in the chains of his lover as he also finds glory by submitting to her will.

This despotic woman forced her husband to make a choice between her and her rival, for she knew well the height of her power and she desired to achieve absolute rule, consolidating her victory with the tears of another.

I endeavored to describe the lamentable woman's condition to her husband and to move him to pity, but in vain. He responded with surprising indifference that the woman was in need of nothing and that she would be happy as in the past. What could I say when he reduces a woman's contentment to the fulfillment of a series of material needs? Of course someday he will regret the weakness of his heart, but time will have passed.

That graceful being who had captured my attention so much with her beauty and delicacy inspires something like antipathy in me now, for I judged her accurately from her words and actions and I am convinced that she would resort to any means with complete mercilessness in order to achieve her intentions.

Mayda to Mme Sira

My Dikran has arrived—he is mine at last. One day I was seated on the embankment, looking at the sea. It seemed that waves of hope were tumbling and all of nature was celebrating my fortune, so beautiful was everything and merry. Suddenly a bird began to warble and I was listening to it enraptured—at times it would release a cry and immediately fall silent, and at other times it would shower pearls of harmony. Suddenly another sound responded to it; a hearty accompaniment began between them that was obviously the indulgence of two loving beings. For birds, as for people, the music of joy and love are the same. In misery, as well as in contentment, any friend is a consolation. In the first case, it is as if the pain is relieved, and in the second, joys are doubled. So I was looking all around to find that nest of love, when suddenly I saw Dikran dashing toward me, arms spread out. I let out a cry, my eyes dampened, I thought that joy was going to kill me.

"Mayda, Mayda!" he said, "Is it truly you? Or are my eyes deceiving me? Say something so that I hear your voice!"

"Dikran!" I responded, "my happiness is overtaking me."

"Unlucky being!" he murmured, "It is clear that you are intensely troubled. But your sorrows have given you a more melancholic beauty."

Traces of pain appeared sealed on his face as well. He wanted to immediately hasten our marriage, but I opposed it in honor of his deceased wife. "Always noble and noble in everything," he said.

Perhaps you will condemn me, my dear, pointing out that I seek causes for anxiety. But it is true that perhaps I became the cause of another's death, and I braid my happiness with the yellowed flowers of her youth. Did that poor being curse me, if not with words then at least with her heart? And didn't she have the right to utter a curse on the person who was robbing Dikran's heart from her? But this thought does not trouble the contentment of my heart; like a light cloud in my bright sky, it only dulls the sun a little. All my memories of pain are so erased that it seems that I bear no grief. It is as if my soul is an enduring piece of music whose final notes will cease in the lap of eternity.

Oh, how lovely is life when the heart is full of joy! Dikran is a guest of Levon, but spends almost all his moments with me. We never recall our sad past, we only smile at the future, full of hope. It is as if I am being reborn and I wish to have an eternity to worship my Dikran. I am suffering from a light cough and, every time I cough, he looks at me terrified and sorrowfully murmurs, "My poor child!" At one time I would think that life was fleeing from me, whereas now I am all strength and health. I want to live. No, no longer do I want death whose help I was plaintively begging for.

In my rejoicing, however, a foreboding, menacing shadow passes before me. Terror has overtaken me, and it seems that the beating of my heart has ceased for a moment. One day, when I was swimming in such fortune, it must have appeared that the veil of sadness was draping my face, for Dikran, perturbed, asked me what was going on. "Oh!" I responded, "That woman, that foreboding spirit that burns for our perdition, will she tolerate our bliss? Where is she now, what has she in store for us? Perhaps she is working in the dark toward the destruction of our happiness. Can I rest as long as she is free?"

"The heavens as my witness," Dikran exclaimed, "if I were ever to get my hands on that malicious woman, I myself would decide her fate, even by taking my vengeance with my life. She has to pay with drops of blood for each tear you shed."

"How do you mean, Dikran?" I asked. "You want to stain your hands with blood?"

"What are you saying?" he responded. "I would save the world from a monster who can create new victims every day. In this case murder is a virtue, for I destroy one life in order to save many."

Mayda to the Count

Dikran's wife died. The catastrophe of that unlucky being returns Dikran to me. My joy would be great if I did not remember your affliction. Why should a noble person like you have pain alone as his lot, and why should I be powerless to make you the happiest of men?

Listen to me, Count. You had a sister, now you have a brother as well. Don't think of yourself as orphaned on this earth, for two hearts have a place for you. Two hearts will always follow you everywhere and are always ready to serve you. O Count, I loved you with melancholic friendship and now I love you with rejoicing. It seems that joy intensifies our feelings, although the gratitude I had toward you was itself unlimited. So, Count, lodgings, a brother, and a sister impatiently await you on the shores of the Bosphorus.

Mme Sira to Mayda

The depth of my friendship is so familiar to you that you can easily understand the sheer joy the change in your condition causes in me. Get married as soon as possible, do not sacrifice moments of rejoicing to frivolous propriety. Delays are not pleasant for me, and I particularly dislike abandoning to the blows of chance what is sacred, even for a day. Nothing is certain. Insignificant reasons can give rise to difficulties that, passing from obstacle to obstacle, keep one distant from one's intention. Seeing things through is the most secure means for achieving what we desire. I consider the present to be a sincere friend who shows clearly what is before my eyes, while the future is always doubtful and I always await an unpleasant circumstance. Never sacrifice what is secure now for potential gain. Be wary of days, hours, and even seconds, for sometimes one second conceives a world of events, transforming everything, throwing things off, and frustrating the best calculations.

The enchanting despot left for a few days. I do not know how her husband agreed to this separation, though it be brief, for this man is so bewitched by that woman that even the sunlight seems to lose its luster without her. To be enraptured by what charms her, to be elated with her, to rule with her, to fulfill her capricious wishes—this is his life.

Some women are a plague on humanity, for they are an evil power before which everything bows. And that power is not due to beauty alone, but rather to the intellectual abilities that accompany it. Beauty is a really irresistible force, but it does not last long without subtlety, intelligence, and ingenuity to assist it. And those who have had great and lasting success in this world owe it to moral, intellectual, and hidden, or revealed means accompanying their graces. Beauty is a fire that is extinguished when the mind does not stoke it. Coming to my neighbor, she

140

has gathered the advantages of her face and mind, and if she were to have free rein for her activities, who knows what catastrophic intentions she would choose for her capabilities?

Her absence brought me content, and I will gradually cut back my relationship with her, for I do not forgive her cruel behavior regarding her poor rival. When I told her of your coming marriage, this news took her by great surprise. She seemed especially displeased when I first gave her a brief overview of your love story. An evil heart is grieved by the success of others—this is a very well-known matter.

The Count to Mayda

Fortune smiled upon you once again. Be happy, Mayda. Do not eclipse your pure joy with any bit of sadness by remembering me. Be happy with the one chosen by your heart—this is my satisfaction. I had one intention since knowing you, that is, to serve you, to soothe the bitterness of your life, to support you in your moments of despair, but my responsibility ended before it began. You no longer have any need of me, for deserving hands are ready to help you. A noble and selfless heart stands in your defense. I do not wish my life to remain completely useless, so I will go to a remote country to serve humanity gone astray. With my efforts and capabilities, I will join the servants of humanity who have taken on the responsibility of softening the morals of wild and barbarian peoples, conveying the miracle-working idea of God to them, making them familiar with social life, and ultimately making human those who live a brutish life.

The benefit of humanity will be my only pleasure on this earth after the pleasure provided by your happiness. If I fall victim to my undertaking, do not cry over me, because I will be the martyr of humanity and I consider that martyrdom a glorious fate. At that time I will charge you with my memory as of a brother. Be happy, Mayda! This is the only wish that remains for me. Tell your Dikran that he has a friend in me and that I hand over to him the care of your precious life. When this letter reaches you, my life will have already become the plaything of the sea. When I have the occasion, I will send word to you, like a far echo from someone near death. If a single line from you were to reach me one day at my desolate place, oh, I would find the world once again!

Farewell, Mayda, my beloved sister!

Mayda to Mme Sira

Our wedding took place in complete silence in the presence of a few guests. My life is a crystal clear ray of light. Happiness flows through my veins. I live in rapture. A new being has been born in me. If I was consigned to inactivity for some time, if I was useless for all, if my state of affairs was aimless, today I have a purpose: to devote my days to Dikran and the rest of my time to the nation. When people are happy, they wish to serve everyone and to satisfy everyone. And who has more right to my sympathies than my nation, to which I would like to dedicate the contributions of my happy heart? But I will always maintain a fondness for you, who managed to soar safely through storms and tempests.

I don't know yet how long we will continue to live in Constantinople. But it is certain that we will come to visit you because it is your right to be valued and loved by that person who has become my companion in fortune. You have a right to our everlasting gratitude, for you have been a guide in my life and a consolation in times of grief. And the absence of that beautiful acquaintance of yours causes me no sorrow at all. You already know that I never had any sympathy for her. She reminds me of Herika in miniature, acting in a limited capacity.

But before I leave, I want to make arrangements for an idea that Dikran and I had in the early period of our relationship; to establish a workroom (*ouvroir*)[6] for women in a populous section of Constantinople, with the support of the newly formed Women's Society, where the needy women of the district may find a secure means of livelihood.

Poverty is relieved by work—a comparatively comfortable life comes into being, each person begins to look for strength within, to respect themselves, to rise, to contemplate the idea of independence, to think and act as a free person, and finally to cease being an animal and to become a human being. So this workroom can serve two purposes; one, to relieve poverty by bringing about a love for work, and the other, to put an end to laziness. The Armenian woman has a particular aversion to work—she considers it disrespectful to herself, an insult to her dignity. Whereas to live at the expense of some other, to be a burden to another, to be nourished by secret alms, namely to submit to the whims of others or to live under obligation, she considers all of this to be very natural and becoming. It follows that the idea of personal freedom has undergone various levels of destruction among us.

Before leaving, I have proposed as a modest start to set up the foundation for this work, leaving to time and diligent workers the future expansion of activities.

I consider it superfluous to tell you the details of this idea of mine. I presented the activity in its basic form and I am sure you applaud such a beginning. The result will be the relief of misery and the beginning of work through which people can reach their potential.

Mme Sira to Mayda

The realization of your beautiful dreams is the completion of my desires. Finally your fate has been given over to worthy hands and I can die with a heart at peace. I demand to see you with your husband and to make the acquaintance of that person who now assumes the care of such a favored being as yourself.

I congratulate you on your idea of establishing a workroom. The centers of work being reduced among us, each needy woman, without a pang of conscience and without feeling any shame, resorts to begging after claiming lack of work. To relieve poverty as well as laziness, to encourage work with work, is to partly heal the open wounds of society. Such an undertaking is truly worthy for those who have hearts and minds. The most beautiful service to society is to nourish people not with alms, but with the fruits of their own labor; laziness is the destruction of the human state and the onset of servility before one's benefactor, for each handout encourages slavery. The hand that gives is simultaneously the hand that binds as well. The more benefactors, the more despots. The more recipients, the more prisoners.

Work—through which people are ennobled—is not respected by the Armenian woman because she has no idea of personal freedom. She looks for her contentment in material gain, for she is ignorant of the fact that she is meant for a moral and intellectual life, to think and act freely. Work leads to a comfortable life, a comfortable life to independence, independence to progress. We need progress more than other nations because we are so far behind in the vast family of enlightenment.

The organization of societies, that is, bringing together individual strengths, is the surest way to operate. By multiplying the number of societies, progress will be palpable. But establishing them is not enough—it is necessary to fortify them as well, for creating is the present, fortifying is the future.

For a few years now, societies keep on multiplying among us. Organizing them is a difficult responsibility, for they are a novelty, and whatever is new seems suspicious. The results of successful groups inspire trust and confidence by which people are willing to offer their small contribution without reservation. Armenians are still not accustomed to gladly support progressive or philanthropic undertakings. Their support is very often a sacrifice for their prestige or the result of a pang of conscience. In any event, beginnings are difficult, and that responsibility becomes a heavy burden on the first workers of the nation. Patriotic feeling is only a word now. When that word turns into a feeling, and the feeling comes to light—then progress is made, and then the young nation reaches its age of reason and becomes destined to thrive.

Poverty and ignorance are fatal diseases that consume humanity, while work and enlightenment push it forward, displaying its magnificence. The life of nations is comprised of the serious and enduring entirety of individual activities. Thus, to refuse any contribution, even the smallest—an atom—is a theft harmful to that general, gradual activity. It is a crime against the nation.

Life entails the marshaling of intellectual and moral capacities. Who has the right to condemn to immobility, loss, or death something which is meant for acting, for bearing fruit, and for enduring? That is ethically murder, for people are responsible for themselves, their conscience, and the company they keep. Nowhere is there as much to do as within the nation that wants to toss off its dark past and to live the bright life of great nations. For everything is to be destroyed in order to be reconstructed; the first workers will become the martyrs of their labor, and they too will remain ruins piled beneath ruins. The act of destroying is difficult and reconstruction even more so. The spirit of resistance, darkness, and competition all appear because of the lack of experience. And from the collision of opposing passions, from the struggle between night and light, the monster of disorder is born. Whatever was beginning to sprout, hatch, rise, or live would be condemned to perdition, and it would be necessary once again to go back to a work which had begun, being subject to the same difficulties, dangers, and struggles. It will be necessary to hand over the continuation of this undertaking to others, as well as the responsibility to emerge victorious in a lasting way and in desperate competition.

It is the duty of each generation to leave some work for progress to the following generation. Yes, it is the sacred duty to take a step towards progress. Woe to that generation that, its arms crossed across its chest, idly looks around and answers "nothing" to the future demanding an account for the use of its time. The lazy state of affairs of that indolent generation is a theft of time, a robbery of progress. There is so much to do. The ruins of the past are to be swept away, whatever is done is to be consolidated, and accomplishments are to be brought to a head. Time is precious. We are the last invitees to the banquet of enlightenment. It is necessary that we prepare our places and take them in an appropriate manner. However great the responsibility, equally large will be the needed selflessness and sacrifice. Consequently, negligence and powerlessness are equally condemnable.

National progress is in jeopardy. The future generation is approaching. It will curse us if we meet it with empty hands. There is no need to be frightened by difficulties—rather we must act and continue to act, to descend until we reach the final step on the staircase of humanity, the masses (*plèbe*).[7]

The masses are the smelling rags that have cots for beds during the night and hunger for company during the day. The masses are the fetid crowds that need bread and, leaning upon one another, extend their heads toward joyous humanity as a grotesque mal-nourished specter. An unnatural flicker enlivens them, for that is the basest expression of humanity. But if a struggle or a revolution emerges, their vital dregs burst out brutally at that time, and they spread over society all their despair, insolence, brutishness, and indignation long since gathered and hoarded because of their hunger and poverty.

Work should penetrate those rags, putting an end to hunger. Light should spread in that nest of darkness. A soul should be awakened in that human flock who, when given the ideas of its essence and capacities, can urge crowds that have been corrupted by the fetid smell of moral immobility, and can move them and spread life there. Nobody is occupying themselves with these miserable and unknown martyrs of life who arrive, pine away, and pass by without attracting the attention of a single person. It is the mire that slides and disappears, leaving behind a black trace that is easily wiped out.

We occupy ourselves with almost everything, we take a peek at everything. But who has the courage to approach the foul-smelling masses without disgust, to see meagre bodies that have wasted away beneath rags, and to recognize them as brothers and sisters?

Mayda, lower your eyes towards the crowds, act for them, give them work, be a ray of hope, raise your voice, and draw public attention to those noxious places where helpless humanity is tormented and dies without bread and without fire. Establish a society for them, collect their feeble children—those black flowers of misery who, I say again, know of life only hunger during the day, the ground for a bed at night, and cold during the winter. Make a shelter for them. Let the heirs of misfortune have at least a place to stay so that they may find a piece of bread during the day, a flicker of fire to warm their bodies broken by the cold, and an intellectual spark to illuminate their minds, so that they may finally find the spirit of mercy beneath the human form. Instead of drying up, becoming emaciated, and dying in torture, instead of growing into social sores day by day and corrupting the atmosphere of humankind, let those little beings progress, let them work, let them think. Instead of darkness, let there be light. Let death produce life. Then the living mass that was considered lost to society will create a new source of strength. It will add to its work, it will increase its ability to think, and it will multiply the number of souls to feel, love, pity, and serve.

Evil is to be uprooted. The masses are the evil that grows in constantly infected waters, spreading its poisonous breath everywhere. So descend there and you will heal by relieving, you will wipe out the fundamental disease. No disease cures itself by staying in the same condition. It needs a breath, a soul, in order to find the cure. Be that breath, that soul, Mayda! Join with other breaths, other souls, clean out the foul stench, and render the skeletal human a living human being.

Mme Sira to Mayda

What is this lengthy silence of yours? Does the satisfaction of your heart make you forget your friends so much that you won't sacrifice even a moment for them?

My Turkish neighbor is sunk in despair because it has been confirmed that his adored beauty has come to a catastrophic end, though we never received news of the details.

Though I do not have great confidence in their persistence, it is painful to witness the tears of men. Their pain is powerful but brief, while that of women lasts much longer—it sometimes continues until death, even if we do not have numerous visible examples of these cases. The excessive sorrow of men, if persistent, leads them to murder. And if that feeling recedes, it fades away very quickly. It is true that women do not put an end to their lives, but pain plows a black furrow in their hearts which only time can relieve.

Suicide is a momentary, pitiable bravery that puts an end to unbearable torture. But to live in order to suffer is the heroism of life—it is the strength to compete, to struggle. It is even the quality of rising above suffering. By committing suicide, people become vanquished by misery and, by living, the conquerors of misery. To bear a life full of grief is to stand as a spectator before time which pours drops of bitterness in our cup of life with each moment. And we continuously draw from that cup until we reach its dregs, however much it is filled. This conduct of ours is a continuous martyrdom; it is to resign ourselves to a condition that raises humankind ever higher.

———◦ ◆ ◦———

Mayda to Mme Sira

So you thought that I could forget you—you nearly received word of my death. I owe my life to Dikran. He bestowed a sad gift upon me.

We passed the few days following our wedding at times on boat rides, at times taking shelter beneath the leafy shade on the verdant Asian shores. We rested there so many times, silently worshipping each other, while our hearts loudly spoke and we looked in amazement upon that joyful scenery, the language of which can be discerned only by happy souls. My glance would plunge into Dikran's eyes and I would bless God for giving me life, that is, His most beautiful gift. We were enjoying everything with enchantment—God, who filled eternity with His essence, the sunbeams that caressed the plants, the trees that sheltered the love nests of happy birds, the flowers—those sweet-smelling smiles of nature, the waves that were expressing fury in their foaming.

Ultimately, we found inexhaustible pleasure in everything, for the book of nature is so vast that we were reading love and happiness on each page. This joy of ours was so great that it could not last, of course. It was the bright spring dawn that thick clouds suddenly covered. Does it fall to my lot to know good fortune only in order to mourn its loss? Hardly is a smile outlined on my lips than the finger of mourning wipes it away mercilessly. Are the bitter drops from my eyes necessary for the ocean of humanity's tears? The flower of joy is unable to take root in me, no, for it needs sunlight, whereas I am a starless night, alas!

One day, we went again to the seaside seeking some refreshment beneath a tangled tree, for although it was autumn, we were burning with intense summer heat. It seemed that I was out of breath, and the difficult rising and falling of my bosom was a manifestation of my troubled internal condition. All of Dikran's efforts to provide a bit of relief remained fruitless. It was as if an iron hand was relentlessly crushing my heart, disturbing the peace of my thoughts.

Then I noticed a woman in Oriental garb calmly moving in our direction, and all of a sudden she attacked me with a knife, intending to kill me. Dikran stopped the blow and, snatching that knife, drove it deeply into that woman's heart. She let out a cry that chilled my blood and fell to the ground, with blood flowing from her wound. Dikran pulled the white veil away from her face and I saw before me—O heavens!—Herika. Dikran recognized her and exclaimed, "Justice has been served, my dear Mayda! I took your revenge."

But she looked at me and said with a beastly smile, "I was never deprived of your news, thanks to your friend, Madame Sira. I could have lived safely and without fear like a princess on Corfu with a wealthy husband. But that did not please me, for the idea of your good fortune was unbearable, such that each day a hell seemed to be rolling before my eyes. I left Corfu in order to stop your wedding. But unfortunately I arrived too late, and I will die a double death, leaving Dikran to you."

Her blood was flowing abundantly. I wanted to approach her and help her, for enmity ceases in misfortune. But she signaled to me with a harsh look to stay away and said, "Receiving life from your hands is death." And then she turned her languishing eyes to Dikran and her toughness softened. She looked at him with sorrowful and at the same time loving eyes, and murmured in a weary voice, "Let my blood be your everlasting torment, and my shadow the inseparable companion of your life. At my last moment I don't fear confessing that I always loved you and only you, and I still love you now when your unmerciful hand did not spare me your fatal blow."

"Unfaithful woman!" Dikran exclaimed. "Do you hope to move me to pity with those words and to make me forget the tears that you caused Mayda to shed?"

"Listen to me one last time," Herika said. "If you don't consider the blow you struck me enough because you did not know who I was, here, strike my breast once again, and never have any pangs of conscience. But be sure that I will love you no less. I got to know you for the sake of my misfortune. I wanted to forget your image. I endeavored to bury my love in all sorts of pleasures. But in vain. Because of you, I forgot that I was a woman, I denigrated myself, and I debased myself in prison to the point where I charmed my guard with tears and took shelter in the house of a Turk through him. And thus I die without being able to raise my eyes to the heavens. I die—deserted, insulted . . ."

Her voice faded away and, as she was uttering Dikran's name, she took her last breath. Such a vision was foreboding. My eyes darkened, I don't know what happened. When I came to, I felt that I was lying on my bed. My terror-stricken eyes looked for Dikran. He was next to me waiting, terrified and desperate for signs of life. Oh, why didn't I sleep with the slumber of eternity? What purpose did my awakening serve?

On the day following this disastrous event, Dikran was arrested or, so much the better for me to say, they robbed me of life. Dikran pays for the days he bestowed upon me with the sacrifice of his freedom. A miserable gift!

I went to visit Dikran in prison. I wanted to share his imprisonment, but even that consolation was denied me. Instead of me providing relief to him, he consoled me with assurances that he would soon return to my side once again without the fear of a wicked spirit's plans. He has such a noble air about him that he is magnificent even in prison—nothing debases him, nor does anything depress him. On the contrary, he causes so much deference in the guards that, when they approach him, it is as if they are going to receive orders from him. He looks much more like a judge than a convict. True greatness reveals itself in all circumstances and nothing can suppress it.

Dikran's presence in prison seems infinite to me, and infinity without Dikran is like a prison. How much longer must I count the moments, and how long will each moment cause me pain? A few days ago, time was dashing along on the wings of happiness. Now it has begun to crawl slowly, as before.

Herika's image is constantly in my thoughts. I still see with terror that monstrous look which became so sweet when directed at Dikran. Herika, who ruled everywhere, had become the captive of love. Who knows, had she not been caught up in a dismal love, perhaps she too would have lived to love and to forgive. Although she caused my catastrophe, I confess that her final moments aroused my pity. Today, yet again she separates me from my Dikran, but I am unable to curse her, for she knew all too well the poisonous wounds of love.

Mme Sira to Mayda

So she fooled me, then. She was the snake I tended with my own hands and led to you. Woe to me! So I would have played a role in your death! How would I have survived such a catastrophe? But I am consoled by one thing, my having removed a fatal hand from above your head. Now I understand her interest in news about you and her emotions upon hearing about your wedding preparations, as well as her hurried departure. But Herika cleansed the traces of her evil with her blood. I am not surprised at that woman's fierceness in love, nor her hatred, nor her indifference to death. Extreme natures know no bounds in evil, nor in good. Herika died as a felon—in other circumstances perhaps she may have died as a celebrated woman. People with passionate natures very often get ahead of their emotions, circumstances, and events, unable to limit their power. Especially at times, they become playthings of their intense emotions. It is as if a current swiftly carries them—where? They themselves do not know. Their conduct often depends on circumstances.

I am convinced that people are not born monsters. Circumstances, needs, the direction given by different personalities, the development of those personalities under different conditions, the more or less irresistible pressures of emotions— all these things direct people toward deciding their fate. For instance, love is reborn as a wild feeling and this leads to hatred, bravery to foolhardiness, and selfishness to unjust vengeance. All the noble circumstances that could have served the good become tools for causing evil. How little does a heart need to keep from erring, a mind from becoming disturbed, and people from plunging into a precipice as they wander along winding paths. Sometimes the smallest thing sets the stage for an entire future.

See how the events follow each other and how they connect with one another. If Dikran had not set alight an inextinguishable love, Herika would not have been a murderer, you would not have influenced the Count's feelings of hopelessness, Dikran would not have poisoned the innocent heart of his wife, Bedros would not have made amends for his transgression with his death, and finally Dikran would not have stained his spotless hands with blood. Observe, then, how many transgressions, how many crimes, how many catastrophes arise from a single source—that is, the heart of a woman. Finding the catalyst of events is difficult. But if it were possible, we would see that in most cases personal passions have produced these catalysts, and of these passions, the frenzy of love or ambition is paramount.

For instance, Helen is the reason behind the destruction of Troy, Lucretia for the fall of a kingdom, Verginia for the dissolution of the Roman government of the Ten Men. So too with the daughter of Julian, the Count of Tangiers, whose rape by Roderic provided the occasion for putting an end to the kingdom of the Visigoths.

Similarly the ambition of one person reshapes the world, overthrows thrones, raises new ones, and conceals the land with ruins of heaps of people. This is affirmed by the Alarics, Genserics, Attilas, Tamerlanes, Alexanders, and Napoleons—they left traces of blood everywhere as witness to their campaigns.

One person may cause many individuals to suffer, and thousands are born from a single drop of blood, for nothing remains alone and barren. Rather, everything is linked in chains, bears fruit, moves forward, becomes fortified, and becomes coated with blood, flourishes with blood, emerges victorious with blood, and stands proud. Cities are won with blood, kept with blood, and sometimes taken with blood. Religions were defended with blood, and persecuted. Rome spurted out of the blood of an enemy and a brother.

When the people of Moses were being delivered, the corpses of the Egyptians floated in the Red Sea. The final songs and joyous cries of the royal banquet of Babylon were lost in a lake of blood, as the anathema of hatred of the Carthaginians was extinguished in blood and the final sighs of the death throes of Greece languished in blood. From the blood of Christ, who was preaching sublime brotherly love and reconciliation, arose bloodthirsty Christianity, armed to the teeth. Charles V wrote Luther's name upon his flag in letters of blood.

Washington's independence was born from rivers of blood, and in 1789 the sacrifice of the head of the last Capet avenged centuries-long injustices of feudalism and violence. And, as freedom was born, fragments of the kingdom were fading away, tumbling with a clamor through rivers of blood. Always and everywhere blood. They well know its worth and they shed it without any conscience. They complain about a single drop of blood while they squander myriads. Murder is prohibited whereas massacres are forgiven. On the first point, a guillotine falls to one's lot, on the second, a hosanna. Whatever is murder in judgment is conquest in history. One is condemned for having spilled some little blood whereas the other is celebrated for having drawn out rivers of blood.

Observe and you will see that human history is a series of contradictions. What is forgiven here is condemned there. What is rewarded here is punished there. Since the beginning of time, people have held contradictory beliefs when it comes to their actions and their words. When people match what they say with what they do, when injustice is not carried out in the name of justice, vice is not hidden underneath virtue, and ignorance is not beneath knowledge, then a new era will appear, that is, the era of progress, which will bring about a new humanity with brightened, sparkling light, peace, justice, and equality. But until that moment arrives, how many insatiable ambitions will open up bloodied roads in this world! How many innocents will pay for the transgressions of the guilty! How many hearts will sigh, how many passions will roar! Humanity will yet walk through much blood before finally wiping out that calamitous red seal from its brow.

Primitive man lives on blood. But how is the civilized one nourished? The former can justify himself with his brute tastes, needs, lack of provisions, and ultimately the barbarian environment in which he finds himself. But how can the latter be justified? One unknowingly carries out an evil act, while the other knowingly so. So the first is justified due to his ignorance and the second is condemned for his knowledge. So who is more barbarian? Is it the savage who kills for his personal needs and survival or the civilized one who, perfecting fatal tools, drives them into the breast of humanity, with only ambition, hatred, or revenge in mind?

Whatever strikes and kills and, on the other hand, whatever relieves is perfected. They bless the hand that delivers, but do they curse the hand that kills? They are surprised at the first and are equally surprised at the second. The hand that heals is weighed the same as the hand that ruins. Human beings prepare death and at the same time they also prepare the means to save their victims. Death is either something good or something evil. If it is something good, why are those who are armed against it rewarded? If it is something evil, why do they distribute it so abundantly? So then what is death? Perhaps one and the other. But can the same cause be the principle of both good and evil? What kind of logic would find that acceptable?

How can it be that the human mind—which wants to examine, investigate, clarify all things, and decide upon the limits of everything—has not resolved the serious problem of life and death?

Why does it leave the problem in such a limping and unsteady condition? Why? Because its interests and ambition exhort it to maintain an unclear condition which is necessary for its personal views. Justice has not yet drawn the limits of injustice, so that it can expand or contract them as needed. The history of human injustices forms thick shadows that darken the face of humanity.

Mayda to Mme Sira

Dikran is still imprisoned, although they assure me that in a few days he will gain his freedom. However I fear I may not see that day. Though my condition is miserable, I visited him many times. My presence first fills him with joy, but then he is immediately overtaken by sadness after noticing the effects of an implacable illness upon me. My exhausted strength is enlivened only when my steps lead me to Dikran.

The intense autumn cold has had a noticeable effect on me. My heart alone is free from its blows. Oh, what wouldn't I sacrifice to flee from my merciless illness? But that is impossible. How dreadful is that word, my dear—"impossible"!

I wish to live an eternity with Dikran. Nothing terrifies me as much as death, which will separate me from that worshipped being of mine. So, a cold shroud will cover my ardent heart! A cold shroud for the heart, for the ocean of love, whose depth only God can measure. Heart and shroud—that is, the life and death of love! How can what was life be rendered into nothingness? Even Dikran's voice will be unable to resurrect me from my grave. The heart that loved and the heart that did not love—being and nothingness—will have the same fate, a shroud for both.

O God! What purpose does love serve? After shining upon our lives as a dazzling beacon, if the flicker of its infinite heavenly flames is going to die out in the darkness of the grave—what purpose does love serve if it will come to a complete end?

O God! Without Dikran's love, the heavens themselves do not satisfy me. I'll sacrifice all of Your worlds made of light, all of Your endlessness for one glance from Dikran. But my doubt is not blasphemy, O Lord, for if love ends on this earth, it continues in heaven. I want only a soul to worship You and a heart to love my Dikran in eternity.

My dear, how I languish. I feel that soon I will be away from all of my loved ones—from my Houlianée, a part of my essence; from you, who pampered me as a mother; from the Count, to whom I owe Dikran, for, without him, I would have breathed my last upon the sorrowful walls of a convent, unconsoled and alone.

He has lately sent word. He has the responsibility of a Savior among wild peoples. Human beings must have a noble soul when they work to serve others, as their hearts weep, bleed, and they themselves need consolation. They need to be God or the Devil to trample upon sorrow and to boldly look upon its bloody fragments.

Mme Sira to Mayda

What is this behavior of yours, Mayda? Have you begun now to speak of the abyss of the grave? Why are you so dejected? Isn't your love strong enough to dispel your fears? Why do you proclaim the impossible a verdict? The impossible is the ultimate blasphemy that despair throws in the face of the possible. The impossible is the furious laughter springing from the throat of hell, whereas the possible is the heavenly smile fallen from the lips of hope, the beautifully glittering dawn of a bright spring day. Enjoy the present fully, and illuminate it with the sunbeams of love. What does the future and its dark night matter to you? A moment of pleasure is worth immortality. If you cannot have the eternity of love, at least welcome and enjoy the eternity of love for a moment.

An unfair justice separates you from your Dikran. But because they promise you his freedom, know that the final act of justice is being performed.

A man witnesses the murder of his lover and he fulfills the duty of love's vengeance by killing the murderer. He does it according to the dictates of his heart. And justice—which is a captive of the unjust ways of the law—imprisons the one who punished the murderer, trampling underfoot that natural love of justice for which people endanger their very lives. They shed their own blood when a crime is committed against them or their loved ones.

I am not on the side of capital punishment. Quite the contrary. A ruling for an execution is the seal of shame stamped upon the brow of humanity. Man appears as the executioner of his brother, looking at the drops of his blood with unfazed eyes and listening to his bitter sighs with indifferent ears. What is the result of capital punishment for society? By reducing the number of the guilty, does their source dry up or does it hinder others from being guilty? Of course not, as numerous daily crimes confirm. The life of the guilty must serve the welfare of society; that is, their work must be devoted to that while they are deprived of personal freedom. In this way, not only would people cease being executioners, but also society would benefit, and perhaps the guilty would provide a means for making amends for their transgressions as well as for reforming themselves. Each life has its usefulness and society should reap benefit from every circumstance.

Until today the flow of blood was and is thought to be one of the weapons of social justice. Vice and falsehood hide behind the facade of religion and justice, and this camouflage is frequently used as a dreadful weapon. And truly the pyres of the inquisition emit flames. In the name of justice they give death, in the name of freedom they give chains. Humanity passes head bowed beneath the blaze of inquisition, beneath death, beneath captivity. But one day, interrupting this course, it suddenly stands and extinguishes the religious furnaces, shattering the chains of ignorance with its hands, and only the gallows remain standing, for it still demands human martyrs. And abject humanity walks hunched over before the guillotine.

People have been victims of ignorance for centuries. They stay silent, they obey. But one day, they will roar against it, and with their martyrdom wipe out the traces of injustice and prejudice which they are unable to wholly uproot. These injustices and prejudices continuously sprout, if not with the same strength, but with sufficient power to poison and corrupt society once again.

Mayda to the Count

I do not know if these lines of mine will ever reach you. But I don't want to withdraw from this world without having given you my final words of farewell, because you did so much good to me and in return you suffered only evil. Although I was responsible for that evil, unwillingly, I never did weep before my conscience. Believe that my mind immediately came to seek you out numerous times in inhospitable countries where you bestow life and instead constantly risk death. So it is your destiny to work with ingrates or, much better to say, it is the destiny of sublime souls to sacrifice their peace, wealth, and hearts, reserving martyrdom for themselves alone. O noble brother of mine, how sweet a consolation it would have been if, as I was breathing my last, I would be sure that no one would be miserable because of me. But is such a relief forgivable for me? My life was very much ruined by sorrow, and nothing could restore it. Yet again, for the last time, my heart now directs to you a weak echo of deep gratitude. Oh, how grievous it is to be separated from loved ones! So farewell, noble brother, farewell! Would that my memory could fulfill the responsibility of a kindred spirit in your suffering!

Dikran to Mme Sira

I have a sad responsibility to fulfill, Madame, which is to inform you that our Mayda is no more. She asked me to express to you one last time yet again the assurances of her gratitude for your steadfast friendship which had been the support of her afflicted life. The friendship she had with you was great, and you well know that few have been able to love with so much selflessness and elevation of the soul as she did. She requested that I convey to you at once the final heart-rending circumstances of her life, and I obey that hallowed command.

Eight days after Mayda visited me in prison, I was free and returned to her. I am unable to describe her joy. She had forgotten the merciless disease consuming her and, placing her hands in mine, her eyes fixed upon mine, she would murmur, "I am happy," in a faint voice. I looked at her with despair. I saw that I was unable to free her from the clutches of death, and I warmed her cold hands with my unrestrained tears.

"Dikran," she said plaintively, "your sorrow is crushing my soul. Take courage, for our separation will be brief. We will unite above," she added, pointing to the sky, "and nothing will keep us apart. Trust in God, for God helped me in my suffering. He returned you to my love, and now He will give me the courage to be separated from you. Tell me, what would I have done if He hadn't brought you back to me? How could I die without seeing you? My eyes would have closed in mourning, releasing their final despairing glances."

"So you want to leave me an orphan in this world, Mayda?" I called out in a broken-hearted voice. "No, I don't want to live! I will come with you, we will have the very same grave."

"Take heed," she said, "I forbid it, for you will disturb my death's rest, and in my grave I will see once again with foreboding drops of blood that once terrified me. No, Dikran, you will not act that way. I urge you to live in order to love my memory. Swear it to me," she added, "if you want me to die content."

Alas! Could I deny her that?

One day, as her weakness was intensifying, she wanted her room to be decorated with flowers and take on a cheerful appearance. She wore a white garment and was lying on her bed, near death. She looked at the sea, which was sparkling with light. She looked at the final dried leaves of autumn that were to share her lot. She noticed the bird which was singing for her for the last time. Finally she saw all of nature which seemed especially shining with an unusual beauty. Sighing, she said, "How enchanting nature is and how charmingly everything smiles!"

Houlianée and I stood next to her. One of Mayda's hands was in hers, the other one was in mine. She looked at us with loving eyes and then said to her daughter, "My dear Houlianée, give me one last kiss and promise to be a selfless sister to my orphaned Dikran." Houlianée kissed her, made the promise, and rushed out of the room in order to hide the wails that were stifling her.

I was left alone next to Mayda, and I gathered all my courage to restrain my despair.

"O you my adored Dikran," she said, "remember me as much as the sea has waves, the sun has rays of light, the bird has songs, and your heart beats. Remember me. The feelings I have for you have become a religion, and I take this religion with me. If you hear in the silence of the night a voice murmuring, 'I love you,' in your ear, know that it is my voice, which, though dead for everyone, will remain living for you."

I lost my mind. I fell to Mayda's feet, and I covered her frigid hand with tears. She pulled me to her heart and gave up her soul in my arms.

I returned to reality from my loss of sensation only to affirm the bottomless depths of my misery. And now I don't know if I am alive. Madame, you lost a singular friend, and I—my entire world.

Translator's Note

T he list of thank-yous for this translation is not a short one. First of all, I must convey my gratitude to the Armenian International Women's Association for providing me with this opportunity, which is nothing short of an honor and a privilege. I hope the text, with insights and editing, conveys the meaning and spirit that Srpuhi Dussap intended.

In order for that to happen, however, some essential resources were necessary. These included a few scanned and searchable dictionaries at Nayiri.com, specifically the *New Dictionary Armenian-English* by Fr. Madatea Bedrossian (Venice, 1875) and *A Practical Dictionary Armenian-English* by Z. D. S. Papazian (Constantinople, 1905), among others. I would like to take this opportunity to thank my friend Serouj Ourishian, who has made the effort of providing this invaluable treasure trove to the world. It is truly indispensable.

Also, the Armenian version of Wikisource includes the electronic text of *Mayda*, transliterated into Soviet-era orthography. This was vital to maintain consistency throughout. I also made use of Wiktionary and Thesaurus.com to double-check on words or offer meaningful alternatives when relevant. I was fortunate to be provided scanned copies of both the original 1883 edition of *Mayda*, as well as the 1924 reprint, which was useful on occasion to compare and confirm unclear words or sections.

Translation is challenging inasmuch as it is meant to be both technical and creative. Something new comes out in the end—that cannot be helped. Each language is its own world, after all. The process is a re-telling, a re-creation every time.

Dealing with Dussap's language was perhaps the most fascinating aspect of this book. She writes in a Western Armenian from 1883 with vocabulary and grammatical constructions that are archaic, apparently transitional from the classical language to one of the two modern forms. Thankfully, it was rare to find any passage that was outright incomprehensible. Still, I wonder about a few phrases and clauses here or there. It is said that the past is a foreign country, and so one might expect the language of the past to be somewhat strange as well.

But the substance of the text had so many points with which one could easily identify today. There are passages in *Mayda* that condemn social ills such as discrimination between the sexes or polygamy. There are entire paragraphs about how Armenians and Armenia are held back by some children of the nation. The section in which Madame Sira laments that people talk too much and act not enough or where Mayda conceals from the Count the corruption and ineptitude at Armenian institutions in Constantinople—these bits I translated while nodding in acknowledgment. It doesn't matter that a century and more has passed, with wars and genocide in between.

A challenge for me in translation was avoiding the gendered English language, in particular the third person pronouns of "he" and "she." Armenian does not have that distinction. At many points, I purposefully chose neutral terms, such as "human beings," "people," or "humankind" (as opposed to "mankind"), and very often rendered sentences written in the singular to the plural to agree with the neutral "they." Perhaps I was being overly sensitive, aware that I was translating a feminist book, but I felt that this approach conveyed the sense more accurately. There were places where things could not be helped, however, and in many passages Dussap herself clearly meant to speak of men and women separately. All errors and imperfections in the translation are, of course, my own.

The nationalism in *Mayda* is one of the major elements in the text that I found captivating. As Dussap herself states in her Preface, this book is not meant to be a page-turner or grand work of literature. But the ideas it contains are fascinating, especially for 1883. I was astonished to discover that, for Dussap, the struggle for the rights of women and the struggle for the rights of the nation were equated. Today, feminism is stereotypically seen as anti-national or cosmopolitan. But it seems that, once upon a time, the value of the woman as the bearer, educator, and driving force of society—half the population, to state the obvious— was viewed through this nationalistic prism. It is ironic that the kind of progressive role foreseen in this book does not find its adequate echo in society in Armenia today, where nationalism is interpreted from a much more strictly patriarchal point of view.

I hope that, with the help of AIWA, this text manages to shed light on a past era that is perhaps not so past after all, while at the same time illuminating future possibilities.

—Nareg Seferian

Endnotes for *Mayda*

1. "Hissar" is Turkish for "fort." There is one on the European side of the Bosphorus, known in Turkish as "Rumelihisarı," and the other on the Asian side, known as "Anadoluhisarı." (p. 21)

2. The word Տաճիկ [Dajig] used in this paragraph can mean specifically "Turk," perhaps "Arab," or more broadly "Muslim." It is translated as "Turk" throughout. (p. 21)

3. It is interesting to note Dussap's use of Հայաստանցի [Hayasdantsi] here, capitalized, a word meaning "native to Armenia," rather than Հայուհի [Armenian woman]. (p. 104)

4. For Janissaries, Dussap uses the Turkish Էէ՛ուիշէրի [yenicheri]. They were the troops immediately responsible to the sultan, formed in the 14th century as an elite corps comprised of slaves or kidnapped Christian boys, converted to Islam, loyal to the throne. Over the centuries the Janissaries became a corrupt institution, revolting and dominating palace politics on numerous occasions. Sultan Mahmud II had them forcibly and violently disbanded in 1820. (p. 119)

5. The Palaeologues were the last ruling dynasty of the Byzantine Empire. (p. 120)

6. For "workroom," Dussap specifies the French in parentheses as *ouvroir*, giving it the designation գործատուն in Armenian, literally "work-house." (p. 143)

7. For "masses," Dussap uses the Armenian ռամիկ [ramig], with the French *plèbe* given in parentheses. (p. 146)

English-Language Sources

"Women's Idleness" by Srpuhi Dussap, translated into English by Jennifer Manoukian, *The Armenian Weekly*, December 28, 2013.

Andreassian, Elise, "Srpoohi Dussap: The First Armenian Feminist," in *Ararat Magazine*, Vol. XXIX, No. 4 (Autumn 1986), pp. 9–13.

Arnavoudian, Eddie, "Why we should read . . . *Srpuhi Dussap*." Review of Albert S. Sharuryan, *Srpuhi Dussap: Her Life and Work* (Yerevan State University, 1963, in Armenian). (http://www.groong.org/tcc/tcc-20030519.html).

Hacikyan, Agop J., ed., "Srboohi Dussap," in *The Heritage of Armenian Literature*, Vol III (Detroit: Wayne State University Press, 2005), pp. 399–403

Kalaidjian, Azadouhi Simonian, "Serpuhi Vahanian Dussap: Defining a New Role for Women," in *Voices of Armenian Women*, edited by Barbara Merguerian and Joy Renjilian-Burgy (Boston: AIWA Press, 2000), pp. 162–78.

Rowe, Victoria, *A History of Armenian Women's Writing*, 1880–1922 (London: Gomidas Institute, 2009), especially pages 47–89.

TREASURY OF ARMENIAN WOMEN'S LITERATURE

The Armenian International Women's Association publishes a series of English-language translations of works by Armenian women writers. The main focus is on the pioneering female authors who published their works in either Western or Eastern Armenian. This rich and diverse body of literature is relevant not only to present-day Armenians, but also to all those interested in multifaceted issues regarding ethnic identity, social justice, cultural values, and the evolving roles of women in society.

TITLES IN THIS SERIES

I Want to Live: Poems of Shushanik Kurghinian,
translated by Shushan Avagyan. Bilingual edition. (2005)

Diana Der-Hovanessian, *The Other Voice:*
Armenian Women's Poetry Through the Ages (2005)

Zabel Yessayan, *The Gardens of Silihdar,*
translated by Jennifer Manoukian (2014)

Zabel Yessayan, *My Soul in Exile and Other Writings,*
translated by G. M. Goshgarian, et. al. (2014)

Zabel Yessayan, *In the Ruins,*
translated by G. M. Goshgarian (2016)

Srpuhi Dussap, *Mayda: Echoes of Protest,*
translated by Nareg Seferian (2020)